W9-DEF-492

EXPERIENTIAL EXERCISES IN ORGANIZATION THEORY

EXPERIENTIAL EXERCISES IN ORGANIZATION THEORY

H. EUGENE BAKER III
STEVEN K. PAULSON
University of North Florida

Prentice Hall, Englewood Cliffs, New Jersey 07632

Library of Congress Cataloging-in-Publication Data

Baker, H. Eugene.
  Experiential exercises in organization theory / H. Eugene Baker.
III, Steven K. Paulson.
   p.   cm.
  ISBN 0-13-051229-X
  1. Organizational behavior. 2. Organizational behavior—Problems,
exercises, etc. 3. Experiential learning. I. Paulson, Steven K.
II. Title.
HD58.7.B35   1995   94-16782

Acquisitions editor: *Natalie Anderson*
Project manager: *Edie Riker*
Cover design: *Bruce Kenselaar*
Manufacturing buyer: *Patrice Fraccio*

©1995 by Prentice-Hall, Inc.
A Simon & Schuster Company
Englewood Cliffs, NJ 07632

All rights reserved. No part of this book may be
reproduced, in any form or by any means,
without permission in writing from the publisher.

Printed in the United States of America

10   9   8   7   6   5   4   3   2   1

ISBN 0-13-051229-X

Prentice-Hall International (UK) Limited, *London*
Prentice-Hall of Australia Pty. Limited, *Sydney*
Prentice-Hall Canada Inc., *Toronto*
Prentice-Hall Hispanoamericana, S.A., *Mexico*
Prentice-Hall of India Private Limited, *New Delhi*
Prentice-Hall of Japan, Inc., *Tokyo*
Simon & Schuster Asia Pte. Ltd., *Singapore*
Editora Prentice-Hall do Brasil, Ltda., *Rio de Janeiro*

To our families:
SHIRLEY, JEFF, and SCOTT.
SALLY, GREG, ANDY, and ERIC.

CONTENTS

3 **TECHNOLOGY** *29*

4 **STRUCTURE** *39*

5 **DESIGN** *53*

6 CHANGE 69

7 EFFECTIVENESS 81

8 CULTURE 95

9 CONFLICT 111

10 STRATEGY 125

11 SIZE 145

12 DECISION MAKING *157*

PREFACE

The purpose of this book is to provide the student of college level courses in organization theory with a set of classroom exercises that will illustrate the basic principles of organization theory. There is no such book available, yet the experiential approach is widely used and considered to be very effective for these courses. The book consists of 12 chapters that discuss the most basic and widely covered topics in the field. Each chapter consists of a central focus, such as organizational power, production technology, or organizational culture, with all necessary materials to fully participate in three different exercises. The instructor's manual is crucial to effective use of this book.

Taken together as a set, the three exercises of each chapter will have the following characteristics:

1. Minimal preparation—an exercise that can be used by the instructor with very little lead time, usually no more than 5 minutes' preparation time.

2. Full preparation—these exercises require more time to prepare because they are more complex and/or require advance preparation of materials or special arrangements of the room.

3. Instrument-based—students often gain insights by administering (self or to others) questionnaires that illustrate certain organizational components; each chapter includes a tested instrument, usually one that is considered a standard in the field, and in this way students gain familiarity with professional practices.

Because the college itself is often a very convenient, common setting used in illustrating a basic point, at least one exer-cise in each chapter focuses on the college as the organization to be analyzed.

The exercises have been tested in the authors' classes and are drawn from a variety of sources, including books created for other purposes such as college-level courses on organizational behavior and organizational development and the management consulting profession. Some of the exercises are original creations of the authors and many have been adapted from materials created for related purposes for organization theory courses.

In order to minimize the time necessary to become familiar with the exercises, they are presented in a uniform format. Once the instructor and students become familiar with the format, a minimal amount of time will be necessary to assess the features of a given exercise. This format consists of five parts:

1. ***Purpose*** of the exercise in terms of objectives that can be expected to be attained by the class.

2. ***Group size*** in terms of the maximum and minimum class and sub-group (if used) sizes needed for optimal use of the exercise, although, in many exercises, size is not a critical aspect.

3. ***Time required*** for optimal completion of the exercise, including time needed for debriefing the class and reviewing basic concepts.

4. ***Preparation required***, including all instructor and student (when necessary) activities that must be completed prior to conducting the exercise in class.

5. ***Materials*** needed to conduct the exercise. In most cases, these items are presented as a range of requirements inasmuch as all of the exercises may be adapted to conform to the specific objectives and teaching techniques of the instructor.

The book is intended for junior, senior, and graduate courses in organization theory as traditionally taught in departments and colleges of business, education, public administration, and sociology. The exercises could also be adapted for use in courses in organization behavior and organization development. The book is suitable for management training programs aimed at middle and top level managers.

ACKNOWLEDGMENTS

In a very direct sense, we are grateful for the help that our students have given over the past two years in providing feedback about various versions of the exercises in this book. We could not have done the project without their help. The University of North Florida Seed Grants Program provided support for the national study of teaching methods used in college-level organizational theory courses, and without this aid the project would still be in its developmental stages. Along the way, three very competent and enthusiastic people helped to prepare the manuscript; we are especially grateful to Leanna Payne, Betty Geitz, and Kathy Green.

ENVIRONMENT

Exercise 1

Organizational Diagnosis
Of the
College Setting*

I. Purpose

To use organizational theory as a basis for diagnosing and making recommendations about the fit between the environment of a college and the internal structure of that college.

II. Group Size

May be completed individually or in groups of 5 to 7 members each.

III. Time Required

15 to 30 minutes.

IV. Preparation Required

None, other than reading the very brief case (if assigned) prior to the class.

V. Materials

None.

PROCESS

Step 1. Introduction

When assigned by the instructor, answer the questions in Parts I, II, and III.

PART I: ENVIRONMENTAL UNCERTAINTY (EU)

	To little or no extent	*To a slight extent*	*To a moderate extent*	*To a considerable extent*	*To a very great extent*
To what extent...					
... does the government frequently develop requirements, regulations, and policies that directly affect your organization?	☐	☐	☐	☐	☐
... do frequent technological changes or advances make current products or operations obsolete, requiring major changes?	☐	☐	☐	☐	☐
... is there intense competition among organizations in your field?	☐	☐	☐	☐	☐
... do different clients of your organization require individualized attention?	☐	☐	☐	☐	☐
... does the environment your organization operates in change unpredictably?	☐	☐	☐	☐	☐
Add up the checks in each column:					
Multiply as indicated:	$\times 1$	$\times 2$	$\times 3$	$\times 4$	$\times 5$
Add: EU = _____ =	+	+	+	+	

PART II: DIFFERENTIATION (DI)

	To little or no extent	*To a slight extent*	*To a moderate extent*	*To a considerable extent*	*To a very great extent*
To what extent. . .					
. . . do different groups or units operate on very different time lines (e.g., long-range versus short-term)?	☐	☐	☐	☐	☐
. . . do different groups or units in this organization have quite different task goals (as opposed to many groups doing the same or similar things)?	☐	☐	☐	☐	☐
. . . do groups or units in this organization differ in terms of their emphasis or concern for people versus concern for getting the job done?	☐	☐	☐	☐	☐
. . . do groups or units differ in how formal things are (e.g., emphasis on adherence to rules, regulations, and policies, following the chain of command, etc., vs. few formal rules, much informal contact, etc.)?	☐	☐	☐	☐	☐
. . . are there many different specialized units, groups, or departments in this organization?	☐	☐	☐	☐	☐
Add up the checks in each column:					
Multiply as indicated:	× 1	× 2	× 3	× 4	× 5
Add: DI = _____ =	+	+	+	+	

PART III: INTEGRATING DEVICES (IDS)

	To little or no extent	*To a slight extent*	*To a moderate extent*	*To a considerable extent*	*To a very great extent*
To what extent. . .					
. . . are rules and policies an important basis for interunit coordination?	☐	☐	☐	☐	☐
. . . are formal plans a major basis for interunit coordination?	☐	☐	☐	☐	☐
. . . are formal liaisons (individuals or teams) a significant basis for interunit coordination?	☐	☐	☐	☐	☐
. . . are regular meetings and problem solving sessions for mutual adjustment an important basis for interunit coordination?	☐	☐	☐	☐	☐
. . . is there a great deal of formal effort devoted to inter-unit coordination?	☐	☐	☐	☐	☐
Add up the checks in each column:					
Multiply as indicated:	× 1	× 2	× 3	× 4	× 5
Add: ID = _____ =	+	+	+	+	

Step 2. Score Summary

PART I: Environmental Uncertainty (EU) = _____

PART II: Differentiation (DI)   =   _____

PART III: Integrating Devices (IDs)   =   _____

Scores range from 5 to 25 on each scale.

HIGH   =   20–25

MODERATE   =   11–19

LOW   =   5–10

Step 3. Discussion

Examine the diagnostic chart and, based on your answers to the questions in step 2, be prepared to discuss your answers with the class.

1. How many class members have organizations with EU-DI-IDs "fit"?

2. What were the most common types of "misfit"? Why?

3. How would you go about reducing the DI score? Is it easier to change the DI or the IDs score? Why?

4. Is there any way to change the EU score?

---

* Adapted from Sashkin, M. & Morris, W.C. (1984). Instrument: ID Scales. *Organizational Behavior*. Reston, VA: Reston Publishing Company, Inc., pp. 234-238.

Exercise 2

Stakeholder Demands*

I. Purpose

Many factors outside the organization have a great impact on decisions made inside the organization. Most of these factors evolve as the result of interaction between groups with differing views. A clear understanding of these environmental influences can be had by making an effort to understand these differing views. The purpose of this exercise is to develop the ability to consider the views of several external factors, or "stakeholders," while maintaining a primary focus of the organization itself.

II. Group Size

Both individual responses and composite responses of several (2–5) are effective.

III. Time Required

This exercise can be completed in 30 minutes with groups of 3 to 5, although it has been successfully used as an individual project as well.

IV. Preparation Required

None.

V. Materials

None required, although posters or other types of exhibits may be useful if oral presentations of the positions are given.

PROCESS

Step 1. General Strategy

Read the assigned issue case scenario (1–6) in step 2 of this exercise and decide upon a general philosophical approach to presenting your position on the issue.

Step 2. Specific Arguments

Develop a series of specific arguments based on the general strategy developed in step 1.

ISSUE CASES

1. Due to a number of recent injuries and deaths of children many consumer groups have demanded that toy companies recall various products and institute a new safety testing program for those products. The toy companies respond that they already have a large testing and safety program. They further state that all of their products are clearly labeled with the age group that is appropriate for the toy, safety instructions, and a toll-free telephone number that consumers can call with problems and suggestions. They note that the majority of injuries have occurred when the instructions were not followed or when the toys were given to children younger than the age noted on the packaging.

    A. Consumer group view.

    B. Toy industry view.

2. During contract negotiations, the union insists that, now that the company is in good financial condition, the employees must have a large wage increase to close the gap created by previously limiting increases to allow the company to recover its financial health. The company states that, although its condition has improved, if this large wage increase is approved, it will no longer be able to remain competitive in its pricing and will again face financial hardship.

A. Union view

B. Company view

3. One governmental regulatory agency is supporting legislation that will require additional safety restraints in automobiles while another agency is demanding increased mileage and reduced air pollution. The automobile manufacturers argue that these proposed regulations, in addition to those already in effect, will have a disastrous impact on the industry by increasing the initial cost of automobiles and their maintenance costs. In addition to more unemployment resulting from reduced sales, such regulations will reduce the number of families who will be able to afford a car.

A. Government view

B. Automobile industry view

4. A large insurance company is under fire by several groups who have noted that although the company's work force is 70% female, no senior management positions are held by women. The groups state that if some action is not taken to rectify this problem they will start a nationwide boycott of the company. (In the past this type of boycott has worked very well for the groups.) The company maintains that it has made every effort to find women for senior management positions but has not been able to. The vast majority of women employed by the firm are in clerical positions. The company has several educational programs to prepare their employees for management positions, but the programs are only a few years old and it will be several years before participants will be ready to move into senior management.

A. Women's group view

B. Insurance company view

5. Local environmental agencies have filed notice with a steel mill that it can no longer dump its waste into the river that serves as the town's source of drinking water. Some of the pollutants have been linked with increased incidents of cancer in the area. The mill's managers argue that this requirement to find a new method of waste disposal would increase the operating costs so much that, given the strong foreign competition, they would have to close the mill. The local people say that the mill is the major employer in town, and if the mill is closed over half the population will be unemployed. They would rather have jobs and bad water than no jobs.

A. Environmental agency view

B. Steel Mill view

C. Employee view

6. Several airlines serving the same region have suggested that they agree on fares for certain routes. If they continue the current fare war, they will not be able to maintain service to several areas, as only certain routes are profitable enough to continue under such low fare levels. The people in the affected towns strongly support the idea of fixed fares. Government agencies are clear that such an agreement on price is illegal and will fine the airlines involved.

A. Airline view

B. Government view

C. Local town view

* Roger R. McGrath, Jr., *Exercises in Management Fundamentals*. 1985, pp. 187-190. Reprinted by permission of Prentice Hall, Englewood Cliffs, New Jersey.

Exercise 3

Grocery Store Dilemma*

I. Purpose

To explore the relative merits of three approaches to developing cooperative relationships among competing businesses in order to compete successfully against a common external threat to their individual markets.

II. Group Size

At least 3 groups with a minimum of 3 members each.

III. Time Required

Variable, although a minimum of 40 minutes seems to be necessary to meet the objectives of the exercise.

IV. Preparation Required

No advance preparation necessary, although a reading of the relevant sections of *Organizations in Action* would be very helpful.

V. Materials

None.

PROCESS

Step 1. Introduction

Read the section "The Acquisition of Power" at the end of this exercise or other reading as assigned by the instructor from James D. Thompson's widely studied organizational theory of the 1960s, which seems to be just as relevant today as it was almost 30 years ago. (See *Organizations in Action*, New York: McGraw-Hill, 1967.)

Step 2. The Scenario

The instructor will assign you to one of the three grocery stores that are described in "Small Town Scenario." Read the entire scenario.

Small Town Scenario

Situation

You live and work in a small town with three very competitive, small, locally owned grocery stores facing survival–threatening competition from a large supermarket chain that plans to build a super-supermarket in the center of town. You are part of the ownership group of one of these grocery stores. Your group has decided to establish an interorganizational relationship with one or both of the other stores as a means of reducing uncertainty. Still, your organization wants to retain as much decision-making autonomy as possible. You hire a consultant who has reduced the relative payoffs of alternative courses of Interorganizational Relations (IOR) actions. Soon, a member of your group will meet with representatives from the other stores and then privately with the representative of each of the stores. Thus there will be three negotiations in which you will agree to some form of IOR.

The Three Stores:

Americana Grocery Store specializes** in fresh produce but also sells meat and grocery items.

Buddy's Grocery Store specializes in locally butchered meat but also sells produce and grocery items.

Corner Grocery Store specializes in gourmet and ethnic specialty grocery items but also sells produce and meat.

Step 3. Payoff

Familiarize yourself with the following IOR Payoff Schedule and Decision Reporting Format.

The IOR Payoff Schedule

A. If not involved in any IOR==> 0 points

B. If involved in a dyadic IOR:

contract	==>	9 points
co-optation	==>	12 points
coalition	==>	15 points

C. If involved in a triad IOR:

contract	==>	6 points
co-optation	==>	8 points
coalition	==>	10 points

The Decision Reporting Format

Our store, the _____ hereby agrees to enter into a _____ type

of interorganizational relationship with _____ for the purpose of

decreasing competitive uncertainty while maintaining some degree of

autonomy.

** "Specializes" means the store has a long tradition of low prices, high quality, and a wide variety of fresh produce which is the result of of personal relationships outside the organization and the technical knowledge of the owners.

THE ACQUISITION OF POWER

Complex organizations "acquire" dependence when they establish domains, but the acquisition of power is not so easy. Organizations may, however, trade on the fact that other organizations in their task environments also have problems of domain and face constraints and contingencies. In the management of this interdependence, organizations employ cooperative strategies. Organizations avoid having to anticipate environmental action (Prop. 2.4) by arranging negotiated environments.

Cooperative Strategies

Using cooperation to gain power with respect to some element of the task environment, the organization must demonstrate its *capacity to reduce uncertainty* for that element and *must make a commitment* to exchange that capacity.

Thus, an agreement between A and B specifying that A will supply and B will purchase reduces uncertainty for both. A knows more about its output targets, and B knows more about its inputs. Likewise, the affiliation of a medical practitioner with a hospital reduces uncertainty for both. The medical practitioner has increased assurance that his patients will have bed and related facilities, and the hospital has increased assurance that its facilities will be used.

Convincing an environmental element of the organization's capacity to satisfy future needs is enhanced by historical evidence; prior satisfactory performance tends to suggest satisfactory performance in the future and we might expect the organization to prefer to maintain an ongoing relationship rather than establish a new one for the same purpose.

Under cooperative strategies, the effective achievement of power rests on the exchange of commitments, the reduction of potential uncertainty for both parties. But commitments are obtained by giving commitments and uncertainty, reduced for the organization through its reduction of uncertainty for others. Commitment thus is a double-edged sword, and management of interdependence presents organizations with dilemmas. Contracting, co-opting, and coalescing represent different degrees of cooperation and commitment, and present organizations with alternatives.

Contracting refers here to the negotiation of an agreement for the exchange of performances in the future. Not restricted to those agreements that legal bodies would recognize, our usage includes agreements formally achieved between labor and industrial management via collective bargaining, but it also includes the understanding between a police department and minor criminals to forego prosecution in exchange for information about more important criminal activities. It also covers the understanding between a university and donor involving, for example, the naming of buildings or the awarding of honorary degrees. Contractual agreements thus may rest on faith and the belief that the other will perform in order to maintain a reputation or prestige (Prop. 3.2), or they may depend on institutional patterns whereby third parties can be depended on to evaluate fulfillments of obligations and assess penalties for failure (Macaulay, 1963).

Co-opting has been defined (Selznick, 1949) as the process of absorbing new elements into the leadership or policy-determining structure of an organization as a means of averting threats to its stability or existence. Co-optation increases the certainty of future support by the organization co-opted. Acceptance on the corporation's board of directors of representatives of financial institutions, for example, increases the likelihood of access to financial resources for the duration of the co-optive arrangement. But co-opting is a more constraining form of cooperation than contracting, for to the extent that co-optation is effective it places an element of the environment in a position to raise questions and perhaps exert influence on other aspects of the organization.

Coalescing refers to a combination or joint venture with another organization or organizations in the environment. A coalition may be unstable or it may have a stated terminal point; but to the extent that it is operative, the organizations involved act as one with respect to certain operational goals. Coalition not only provides a basis for exchange but also requires a commitment to future joint decision making. It is therefore a more constraining form of cooperation than co-opting.

[Recall that] Proposition 3.3 said that when support capacity is concentrated within few elements in the task environment, organizations under norms of rationality seek power relative to those on whom they are dependent. We can refine that proposition somewhat, using the distinctions just introduced relative to degrees of cooperation and commitment.

Proposition 3.3a: When support capacity is concentrated and *balanced against concentrated demands*, the organizations involved will attempt to handle their dependence through contracting.

Proposition 3.3b: When support capacity is concentrated *but demand dispersed*, the weaker organization will attempt to handle its dependence through co-opting.

Proposition 3.3c: When support capacity is concentrated and balanced against concentrated demands, but the power achieved through contracting is inadequate, the organizations involved will attempt to coalesce.

---

* Adapted from Thompson, J.D. (1967). *Organizations in Action*. New York: McGraw-Hill Book Company, pp. 35-36. Reproduced with permission of the publisher.

POWER

Exercise 4

Political Processes
In Organizations

I. Purpose

To analyze and predict when political behavior is used in organizational decision making and to compare participants' ratings of politically based decisions with ratings of practicing managers.

II. Group Size

Groups of 3 to 7 members each.

III. Time Required

1 hour.

IV. Preparation Required

None.

V. Materials

None.

PROCESS

Politics is the use of influence to make decisions and obtain preferred outcomes. Surveys of managers show that political behavior is a fact of life in virtually all organizations. Every organization will confront situations characterized by uncertainty and disagreement, and hence standard rules and rational decision models cannot necessarily be used. Political behavior and rational decision processes act as substitutes for one another, depending on the degree of uncertainty and disagreement that exists among managers about specific issues. Political behavior is used and is revealed in informal discussions and unscheduled meetings among managers, arguments, attempts at persuasion, and eventual agreement and acceptance of the organizational choice.

In this exercise, you are asked to evaluate the extent to which politics will play a part in 11 types of decisions that are made in organizations.

Step 1. Individual Ranking

Rank the 11 organizational decisions listed on the scoring sheet according to the extent you think politics plays a part. The most political decision would be ranked 1; the least political, 11. Enter your ranking on the first column of the scoring sheet.

Step 2. Team Ranking

Divide into teams of 3 to 7 people. As a group, rank the 11 items according to your group's consensus on the amount of politics used in each decision. Use good group decision-making techniques to arrive at a consensus. Listen to each person's ideas and rationale fully before reaching a decision. Do not vote. Discuss items until agreement is reached. Base your decisions on the underlying logic provided by group members rather than on personal preference. After your team has reached a consensus, record the team rankings in the second column on the scoring sheet.

Step 3. Correct Ranking

After all teams have finished ranking the 11 decisions, your instructor will read the correct ranking based on a survey of managers. This survey indicates the frequency with which politics played a part in each type of decision. As the instructor reads each item's ranking, enter it in the "Correct Ranking" column on the scoring sheet.

Step 4. Individual Score

Your individual score is computed by taking the difference between your individual ranking and the correct ranking for each item. Be sure to use the *absolute* difference between your ranking and the correct ranking for each item (ignore pluses and minuses). Enter the difference in column 4, labeled "Individual Score." Add the numbers in column 4 and insert the total at the bottom of the column. This score indicates how accurate you were in assessing the extent to which politics plays a part in organizational decisions.

Step 5. Team Score

Compute the difference between your group's ranking and the correct ranking. Again, use the *absolute* difference for each item. Enter the difference in column 5, labeled "Team Score." Add the numbers in column 5 and insert the total at the bottom of the column. The total is your team score.

Step 6. Compare Teams

When all individual and team scores have been calculated, the instructor will record the data from each group for class discussion. One member of your group should be prepared to provide both the team score and the lowest individual score on your team. The instructor may wish to display these data so that team and individual scores can be easily compared as illustrated on the bottom of the scoring sheet. All participants may wish to record these data for further reference.

Step 7. Discussion

Discuss this exercise as a total group with the instructor. Use your experience and the data to try to arrive at some conclusions about the role of politics in real-world organizational decision making. The following questions may facilitate the total group discussion.

1. Why did some individuals and groups solve the ranking more accurately than others? Did they have more experience with organizational decision making? Did they interpret the amount of uncertainty and disagreement associated with decisions more accurately?

2. If the 11 decisions were ranked according to the importance of rational decision processes, how would that ranking compare to the one you've completed above? To what extent does this mean both rational and political models of decision making should be used in organizations?

3. What would happen if managers apply political processes to logical, well-understood issues? What would happen if they applied rational or quantitative techniques to uncertain issues about which considerable disagreement existed?

4. Many managers believe that political behavior is more extensive at higher levels in the organization hierarchy. Does this exercise provide any evidence that would explain why more politics would appear at higher rather than lower levels in organizations?

5. What advice would you give to managers who feel politics is bad for the organization and should be avoided at all costs?

Scoring Sheet follows on page 22

SCORING SHEET

Decisions	1. Individual ranking	2. Team ranking	3. Correct ranking	4. Individual score	5. Team score
1. Management promotions and transfers					
2. Entry level hiring					
3. Amount of pay					
4. Annual budgets					
5. Allocation of facilities, equipment, offices					
6. Delegation of authority among managers					
7. Interdepartmental coordination					
8. Specification of personnel policies					
9. Penalties for disciplinary infractions					
10. Performance appraisals					
11. Grievances and complaints					

	TEAM NUMBER						
	1	*2*	*3*	*4*	*5*	*6*	*7*
Team Scores:							
Lowest individual score on each team:							

---

* Reprinted by permission from pages 339-341 of *Organizational Theory: Cases and Applications*, by R.L. Daft and M.P. Sharfman; Copyright © 1990 by West Publishing Company. All rights reserved.

Exercise 5

The Old Man's Power*

I. Purpose

To demonstrate various basis of power.

II. Group Size

Individually.

III. Time Required

20 minutes.

IV. Preparation Required

None.

V. Materials

None.

PROCESS

Step 1. Introduction

Read the following short description of the relationship between an older man and a young boy:

> A young boy, 15 years of age, washes and waxes several cars, sands a wooden deck by hand, and paints the fence and house of an elderly man over a period of several days. Some activities involve working late into the night, and all result in exhaustion. Moreover, the boy performs all the work voluntarily. The elderly man, although of relatively small stature, is no less the taskmaster, demanding strict attention to detail and rigorous adherence to his instructions, allowing no deviation from the prescribed procedure. He is of oriental descent, a maintenance man for a small apartment complex, and his hobby is creating Bonsai or miniature trees.

Step 2. Individual Response

Answer individually the following questions:

1. What could possibly account for this compliance on the part of the young man, when in fact, no compensation has been offered, nor will be, for this work?

2. Would the young man have not been more disposed to spend this time with his friends in pursuit of other, more enjoyable activities, especially in light of the lack of remuneration?

Step 3. Basis of Power

Using the following list, attempt to determine the source of the old man's power over the young boy:

1. **Reward power** is an individual's ability to influence others' behavior by rewarding their desirable behavior.

2. **Coercive power** is an individual's ability to influence others' behavior by means of punishment for undesirable behavior.

3. ***Legitimate power*** most frequently refers to a manager's ability to influence subordinates' behavior because of the manager's position in the organizational hierarchy.

4. ***Expert power*** is an individual's ability to influence others' behavior because of skills, talents, or specialized knowledge possessed by the individual.

5. ***Referent power*** is an individual's ability to influence others' behavior as a result of being liked or admired. (Hellriegel, Slocum, and Woodman, 1992)

Step 4. Group Comparison

Compare your assessment of the source(s) of power of the old man with others in a small group. Attempt to reach an agreement among the group members as to the ***primary*** source of power. Be prepared to provide support for your choice.

---

* Adapted from Baker III, H.E. (1993). Wax on Wax Off: French and Raven at the Movies. *Journal of Management Education*, 17(4), pp. 517-519.

Exercise 6

Unequal Resources*

I. Purpose

This exercise gives participants a chance to observe how groups (1) use resources that have been unequally distributed and (2) negotiate to obtain the resources they need.

II. Group Size

Four groups, each having 2 to 4 members.

III. Time Required

Less than 1 hour.

IV. Preparation Required

Copy 1 task sheet for each group.

V. Materials

Group 1: scissors, ruler, paper clips, pencils, two 4-inch squares of red paper, and two 4-inch squares of white paper

Group 2: scissors, glue, and two sheets each of gold paper, white paper, and blue paper, each 8 1/2 by 11 inches

Group 3: felt-tipped markers and two sheets each of green paper, white paper, and gold paper, each 8 1/2 by 11 inches

Group 4: five sheets of paper, 8 1/2 by 11 inches one green, one gold, one blue, one red, and one purple

PROCESS

Step 1. Introduction

Introduce the exercise as an experience with the use of resources needed to accomplish a task that have been distributed unequally among groups. Form the groups. Groups should be placed far enough away from each other so that their negotiation positions are not compromised by casual observation.

Step 2. Observer Briefing

Meet briefly with the observers and discuss what they might focus on. Any aspect of negotiation and problem solving can be observed.

Step 3. Distribute Materials

Distribute an envelope of materials and a copy of the accompanying task sheet to each group. Each group has different materials, but each must complete the same tasks.

Step 4. Start Exercise

Groups may negotiate for the use of materials and tools in any way that is agreeable to everyone. The first group to finish all the tasks is the winner. Begin.

Step 5. Declare Winner

When the groups have finished, declare the winner. Conduct a discussion on using resources, sharing, negotiating, competing, and using power. Ask the observers to participate in the discussion. Then ask each cluster to summarize its conclusions about the use of power that manifested itself during the exercise.

Unequal Resources Task Sheet

Each group is to complete the following tasks:

1. Make a 3-by-3-inch square of white paper.

2. Make a 4-by-2-inch rectangle of gold paper.

3. Make a 3-by-5-inch T-shaped piece of green and white paper.

4. Make a four-link paper chain, each link in a different color.

5. Make a 4-by-4-inch flag in any three colors.

The first group to complete all the tasks is the winner. Groups may negotiate with each other for the use of needed materials and tools on any mutually agreeable basis.

---

* Adapted from Heisler, W.J. (1978). Admissions Committee: A consensus-seeking activity. In J. W. Pfeiffer and J.E. Jones (eds.). *The 1978 Annual Handbook for Group Facilitators*. San Diego, CA: University Associates, Inc., pp. 15-27.

3

TECHNOLOGY

Exercise 7

Measuring Technology*

I. Purpose

To assess the extent of task variability and problem analyzability present in various organizational units.

II. Group Size

Questionnaire completed individually. Group discussion with 5 to 7 members each.

III. Time Required

Approximately 50 minutes. Questionnaire may be completed prior to class to expedite.

IV. Preparation Required

None.

V. Materials

None.

PROCESS

Task variability and problem analyzability can be measured in an organizational unit by having employees answer the following 10 questions. Scores are normally derived from responses scored on a scale of 1 to 7 for each question.

Step 1. Directions

Complete the questionnaire for each of the following departments:

Computer Operations
(fetching and mounting tapes, printer setup)

Methodology Department
(survey development, survey specifications)

Personnel Training Package Group
(rewrite training materials, update training manuals)

Computer Systems Analysis
(customizing user computer systems)

Step 2. Small Group Discussion

Meet in small groups to discuss and compare individual responses for each department.

Task Variability

The following questions pertain to the normal, day-to-day pattern of work carried out by yourself and the people in your work unit. Please check the appropriate answers.

	Very few of them			Some of them		Most of them	
	1	2	3	4	5	6	7
1. How many tasks are the same from day to day?							

This part includes more questions about the nature of your normal, day-to-day work activities. Please check the appropriate answer to each of the following questions.

	To a small extent			To some extent		To a great extent	
	1	2	3	4	5	6	7
2. To what extent would you say your work is routine?							
3. People in this unit do about the same job in the same way most of the time.							
4. Basically, unit members perform repetitive activities in doing their jobs.							

The following question pertains to the amount of variety you encounter in your daily work. Please check the number that best fits your job.

	Very little			Moderate amount		Very much	
	1	2	3	4	5	6	7
5. How repetitious are your duties?							

Problem Analyzability

The following questions pertain to normal, day-to-day patterns of work carried out by yourself and the people in your work unit. Please check the appropriate answers.

	To a small extent			*To some extent*		*To a great extent*	
	1	2	3	4	5	6	7
1. To what extent is there a clearly known way to do the major types of work you normally encounter?							

This part includes more questions about the nature of your normal, day-to-day work activities. Please check the appropriate answer to each of the following questions.

	To a small extent			*To some extent*		*To a great extent*	
	1	2	3	4	5	6	7
2. To what extent is there a clearly defined body of knowledge of subject matter that can guide you in doing your work?							
3. To what extent is there an understandable sequence of steps that can be followed in doing your work?							
4. To do your work, to what extent can you actually rely on established proced-ures and practices?							
5. To what extent is there an understandable sequence of steps that can be followed in carrying out your work?							

---

* Adapted from Withey, M., Daft, R.L. and Cooper, W. H. (1983). Measures of Perrow's Work Unit Technology: An Empirical Assessment and a New Scale. *Academy of Management Journal*, 26(1), pp. 45-63.

Exercise 8

Athletics and Physical Interdependence Technologies*

I. Purpose

To explore differences in interdependence, coordination, and management among various athletic teams.

II. Group Size

Complete assignments individually. Meet in groups of 5 to 7 members each to discuss analysis.

III. Time Required

15-30 minutes.

IV. Preparation Required

None.

V. Materials

None.

PROCESS

When instructed, complete the following chart comparing baseball, football, and basketball teams.

	Baseball	*Football*	*Basketball*
Interdependence (pooled, sequential or reciprocal)			
Physical dispersion of players (high, medium, or low)			
Coordination (type of coordination)			
Key management job (primary focus of management)			

* Reprinted by permission from page 136 of *Organization Theory and Design*, by R.L. Daft; Copyright © 1992 by West Publishing Company. All rights reserved.

The Thompson Interdependence Demonstration*

I. Purpose

(1) to illustrate the concepts of *pooled*, *sequential*, and *reciprocal* interdependence;

(2) to illustrate interdependence *within* groups, departments, and organizations;

(3) to illustrate interdependence *between* groups, departments, and organizations; and

(4) to illustrate the reasons for spatial and hierarchical priorities based on the level of interdependence among units.

II. Group Size

Groups of 5 to 6 members each.

III. Time Required

45 minutes.

IV. Preparation Required

None.

V. Materials

Movable chairs, if available, will facilitate exercise. An area, such as a hallway, is needed that is out of hearing range for the participants in the room.

PROCESS

Step 1. Select Executive Committee

Two members of the class will be selected to serve as the executive committee for a hypothetical company.

Step 2. Create Groups

The class will be divided into six groups of roughly equal size.

Step 3. Round 1–Round 6

Detailed instructions will be provided by the instructor for each round.

Step 4. Debrief

---

* Adapted from Bluedorn, A.C. (1993). The Thompson Interdependence Demonstration. *Journal of Management Education*. 17(4), pp. 505-509.

STRUCTURE

Exercise 10

College Organization
And the Things People Say!*

I. Purpose

To begin the process of identifying organizational structures (functional, product/market, matrix) through direct comments made by employees. A crucial point here is that the *intended* structure may not be the one that is *felt* or *perceived* by employees. In this area, perceptions are of crucial importance in determining appropriate leadership styles, communication channels, and, especially, organizational designs.

II. Group Size

Unlimited.

III. Time Required

5 to 20 minutes, depending on the length of step 3 discussion.

IV. Preparation Required

None, except to fill out the questionnaire prior to the class meeting in which the results are to be discussed.

V. Materials

None.

PROCESS

Step 1. Introduction

Organizations basically are structured in one of three forms: functional with departments of shipping, manufacturing, sales, etc.; product/market, where the organization is organized according to product such as the Cadillac division or the consumer products division of General Electric; and matrix organization, which is a combination of functional and product/market.

Step 2. Implementation

As requested by your instructor, place an F (functional), P/M (product/market), or M (matrix) in front of the following quotations about a hypothetical college to indicate which kind of structure is most likely to have produced the statement.

_____ 1. "This will be a special unit. We're going to pull faculty out of history, accounting, and law to work on this project."

_____ 2. "This college is out of control, if you ask me."

_____ 3. "Our student population isn't what it used to be. It's changing so fast. You never know what people want anymore."

_____ 4. "It takes university administration so doggone long to get a decision."

_____ 5. "Everything is the same. You can't tell a business major from a education major."

_____ 6. "This setup is great! Every professor has his or her own skills and we don't have to worry so much about coordinating everything."

_____ 7. "I wish we could experiment on new courses, but everyone around here has tunnel vision."

_____ 8. "This way we'll learn about each other's courses. We'll be able to do it all."

_____ 9. "These Ivy Leaguers are all alike. They want more office space and more secretarial people. They think they should have it all."

_____10. "We've got to watch out for duplication. It can happen quite easily when we're organized like this."

Step 3. Discussion Questions

1. Which comments did you identify as functional? What characteristics of the functional structure would produce such comments?

2. Which comments did you identify as product/market? What characteristics of the product/market structure would produce such comments?

3. Which comments did you identify as matrix? What characteristics of the matrix structure would produce such comments?

4. Is structure alone responsible for such comments such as these? Why or why not?

---

* John T. Samaras. *Exercises, Cases, and Readings Management Applications* 1989, p. 77. Reprinted by permission of Prentice Hall, Englewood Cliffs, New Jersey.

Exercise 11

The Apple-Orange Company Structure*

I. Purpose

To stimulate thinking about the fact that there are several different ways to organize work. Managers can often decide what form of organization structure they would like to have. However, each form has certain advantages and some disadvantages associated with it. In choosing a form of organization, a manager is really deciding which set of problems he or she wants to live with.

II. Group Size

Individually or group discussion (2 to 4 members for each group is usually be the most effective).

III. Time Required

10 to 20 minutes.

IV. Preparation Required

None.

V. Materials

None.

PROCESS

Step 1. Introduction

Read the description of the Apple-Orange Company and then answer the questions that follow.

Step 2. Discussion Questions

Based on your own knowledge, guesses, and common sense, do you believe it is possible to "mix apples and oranges" in this case? That is, would your choice of structure be functional or product? Why do you prefer this structure for the case?

THE APPLE-ORANGE COMPANY

The Apple-Orange Company grows and markets apples and oranges in the southeastern United States. Apple-Orange has been in the produce business for the past 50 years and has some of the finest land for growing these fruits. The company has also been quite successful in marketing its product. Until now, Apple-Orange has been a family business run by old John Graves, whose father and uncle started the business. His son Carl has been working as his assistant since Carl returned from Vietnam.

Basically there are three major sets of activities that must be accomplished to grow and market Apple-Orange's products. One group of workers and managers work in the fields, handling the growing and harvesting of the apples and oranges. Another group of workers and managers worked in development research. This group is made up largely of agricultural scientists who attempt to improve the varieties grown and to increase crop yield. Marketing is handled by several sales personnel who call on wholesalers and fruit distributors in the region. The sales staff is very large and has been, like all other employees, very effective.

John and Carl have been managing Apple-Orange without many formal policies and procedures. The company has few set rules, procedures, and job descriptions. John believes that once people know their job, they should and would do it well.

However, Apple-Orange has grown fairly large, and John and Carl believe that it is now necessary to develop a more formal organization structure. They have invited D. J. Blair, a noted management consultant, to help them. D. J. has told them that they have, basically, two choices. One is a functional organization structure and the second is a product-based organization structure. These two different forms are shown in the accompanying figure.

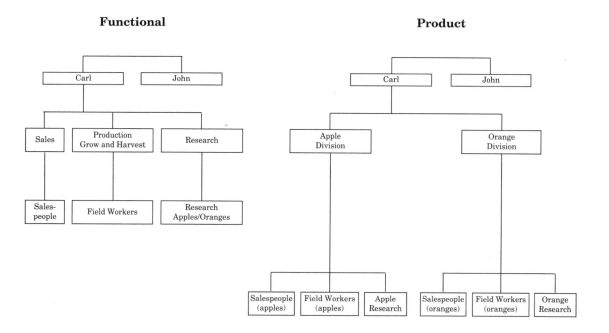

Functional   **Product**

Is your choice of structure Functional? Product? Why?

---

* Adapted from Tosi, H. L. & Young, J. W. (1982). Organizing Exercise 12. *Management: Experiences and Demonstrations*. Homewood, IL: Richard D. Irwin, Inc., pp. 75-79.

Exercise 12

Words-in-Sentences, Inc.*

I. Purpose

(1) To experiment with designing and operating an organization; and
(2) to compare production and quality outputs under different organization structures and/or leadership styles.

II. Group Size

Any number of 5 to 15 person groups.

III. Time Required

The exercise can be conducted in 50 minutes with some advance explanation and group formation so that students can come to class and immediately begin. Otherwise 75 to 90 minutes is required.

IV. Preparation Required

Assembling the materials and locating space that will allow students to work in groups that are spatially separated; movable chairs in one room would be adequate if the room is fairly large; an ideal arrangement would be to have separate rooms with tables to use as work space.

V. Materials

None.

PROCESS

Step 1. Introduction

In this exercise, you will form a "mini-organization" with several other people. You will also compete with other companies in your industry. The success of your company will depend on your (1) objectives, (2) planning, (3) organization structure, and (4) quality control. It may also depend on leadership style. It is important, therefore, that you spend some time thinking about the best design for your organization.

Step 2. Group Formation

Form companies and assign work areas. The total group should be subdivided into small groups of comparable size. Because the success of any one group will not be dependent on size alone, do not be concerned if some groups are larger than others. *Each group should consider itself a company.* Your instructor may designate a manager and give him or her special directions.

Step 3. Detailed Instructions

Read the directions below and ask the group leader about any points that need clarification. Everyone should be familiar with the task before beginning step 4.

Firm and Industry Setting

You are a small company that manufactures words and then packages them in meaningful (English language) sentences. Market research has established that sentences of at least three words but not more than six words each are in demand. Therefore, packaging, distribution, and sales should be set up for three to six word sentences.

The "words-in-sentences" (WIS) industry is highly competitive; several new firms have recently entered what appears to be an expanding market. Because raw materials, technology, and pricing are all standard for the industry, your ability to compete depends on two factors: volume and quality.

Group Task

Your group must design and participate in running a WIS company. You should design your organization to be as efficient as possible during each production run. After the first production run, you will have an opportunity to reorganize your company if you want to.

Raw Materials

For each production run, you will be given a "raw material word or phrase." The letters found in the word or phrase serve as the raw materials available to produce new words in sentences. For example, if the raw material word is "organization," you could produce the following words and sentence: "Nat ran to a zoo."

Production Standards

There are several rules that have to be followed in producing "words-in-sentences." If these rules are not followed, your output will not meet production specifications and will not pass quality control inspection.

1. The same letter may appear only as often in a manufactured word as it appears in the raw material word or phrase; for example, "organization" has two *o*'s. Thus "zoo" is legitimate, but zoology is not. It has too many *o*'s.

2. Raw material letters can be used again in different manufactured words.

3. A manufactured word may be used only once in a sentence and in only one sentence during a production run; if a word for example, *a* is used once in a sentence, it is out of stock.

4. A new word may not be made by adding *s* to form the plural of an already used manufactured word.

5. A word is defined by its spelling, not its meaning.

6. Nonsense words or nonsense sentences are unacceptable.

7. All words must be in the English language.

8. Names and places are acceptable.

9. Slang is not acceptable.

Measuring Performance

The output of your WIS company is measured by the *total number of acceptable words* that are packaged in sentences. The sentences must be legible, listed on no more than two sheets of paper, and handed to the Quality Control Review Board at the completion of each production run.

Delivery

Delivery must be made to the Quality Control Review Board 30 seconds after the end of each production run.

Quality Control

If any word in a sentence does not meet the standards set forth above, *all* the words in the sentence will be rejected. The Quality Control Review Board (composed of one member from each company) is the final arbiter of acceptability. In the event of a tie vote on the board, a coin toss will determine the outcome.

Step 4. Organization Design Phase

Design your organization using as many group members as you see fit to produce your "words-in-sentences." There are many potential ways of organizing. Some are more efficient than others, so you may want to consider the following:

1. What is your company's objective?

2. How will you achieve your objective? How should you plan your work, given the time allowed?

3. What division of labor, authority, and responsibility is most appropriate, given your objective, your task, and the technology?

4. Which group members are most qualified to perform certain tasks?

5. Assign one member of your group to serve on the Quality Review Board. This person may also participate in production runs.

Step 5. Production Run 1

1. The group leader will hand each WIS company a sheet with a raw material word or phrase.

2. When the instructor announces "Begin production," you are to manufacture as many words as possible and package them in sentences for delivery to the Quality Control Review Board.

3. When the instructor announces "Stop production," you will have 30 seconds to deliver your output to the Quality Control Review Board. Output received after 30 seconds does not meet the delivery schedule and will not be counted.

Step 6. Production Review Control Run 1

1. The designated members from the companies of the Quality Control Review Board review output from each company. The total output should be recorded (after quality control approval) on the board or easel.

2. While the board is completing its task, each WIS company should discuss what happened during Production Run 1.

Step 7. Organizational Planning for Run 2

Each company should evaluate its performance and organization. Companies may reorganize for Run 2.

Step 8. Production Run 2

1. The group leader will hand each WIS company a sheet with a raw material word or phrase.

2. Proceed as in step 5 (Production Run 1).

Step 9. Production Review Control Run 2

1. The Quality Control Review Board will review each company's output and record it on the board or easel. The total for Runs 1 and 2 should be tallied.

2. While the board is completing its task, each WIS company should prepare an organization chart depicting its structure for both production runs. If the group had a "manager," what effect did the manager's leadership style have on the group's motivation and production?

Step 10. Class Discussion

Discuss this exercise as a total group. The group leader will provide discussion questions. Each company should share the organization charts it prepared in step 9.

---

* Reprinted by permission from pages 76-79 of *Organization Theory: Cases and Applications*, by R. L. Daft and K. M. Dahlen. Copyright © 1984 by West Publishing Company. All rights reserved.

5

DESIGN

Exercise 13

Bureaucracy and You*

I. Purpose

Two related purposes are intended to be served by this exercise. Because all people seek some degree of order in their lives, the bureaucratic form of organization appeals to all people, but *in varying degrees*. Hence, one purpose is to provide students with the opportunity to assess their own orientation toward bureaucracy. A second purpose is to provide students with the opportunity to assess their own major field of study in terms of orientation toward bureaucracy. Hopefully, these two purposes will serve a larger concern, which is to enable all to develop a broad point of view as to the usefulness of a given organization system.

II. Group Size

Individually only.

III. Time Required

15 to 20 minutes.

IV. Preparation Required

None.

V. Materials

None.

PROCESS

Step 1. Introduction

A person with a bureaucratic orientation is one who is comfortable working in a bureaucracy. Unless the world were populated with people who adjust readily to working for a bureaucracy, organizations such as AT&T or the Ford Motor Co. could not function. Other people, those with a low bureaucratic orientation experience feelings of discomfort working for a bureaucracy. The bureaucratic orientation scale presented next gives you a chance to acquire tentative (not scientifically proved) information about your position on this important aspect of work life.

Step 2. The Bureaucratic Orientation "Test"

Answer each question "mostly agree" or "mostly disagree." Assume that you are trying to learn something about yourself. Do not assume that your answer will be shown to a prospective employer or, for that matter, anyone else.

Mostly Agree	Mostly Disagree		
X		1.	I value stability in my job.
X		2.	I like a predictable organization.
	X	3.	The best job for me would be one in which the future is uncertain.
	X	4.	The military would be a nice place to work.
	X	5.	Rules, policies, and procedures tend to frustrate me.
X		6.	I would enjoy working for a company that employed 85,000 people worldwide.

Mostly Agree	Mostly Disagree		
✕	_____	7.	Being self-employed would involve more risk than I am willing to take.
✕	_____	8.	Before accepting a job, I would like to see an exact job description.
_____	✕	9.	I would prefer a job as a freelance house painter to one as a clerk for the Department of Motor Vehicles.
✕	_____	10.	Seniority should be as important as performance in determining pay increases and promotion.
✕	_____	11.	It would give me a feeling of pride to work for the largest and most successful company in its field.
✕	_____	12.	Given a choice, I would prefer to make $70,000 per year as a vice president in a small company to $80,000 as a staff specialist in a large company.
_____	✕	13.	I would regard wearing an employee badge with a number on it as a degrading experience.
_____	✕	14.	Parking spaces in a company lot should be assigned on the basis of job level.
✕	_____	15.	I would generally prefer working as a specialist to wearing many hats.
✕	_____	16.	Before accepting a job (given a choice), I would want to make sure that the company had a good program of employee benefits.
✕	_____	17.	A company will probably not be successful unless it establishes a clear set of rules and regulations.
_____	✕	18.	Regular working hours and vacations are more important to me than finding thrills on the job.

Mostly Agree	Mostly Disagree		
_✗_	_____	19.	You should respect people according to their rank.
_____	_✗_	20.	Rules are meant to be broken.

Step 3. Scoring

Give yourself a plus one for each question that you answered in the bureaucratic direction.

1. Mostly agree	11. Mostly agree
2. Mostly agree	12. Mostly disagree
3. Mostly disagree	13. Mostly disagree
4. Mostly agree	14. Mostly agree
5. Mostly disagree	15. Mostly disagree
6. Mostly agree	16. Mostly agree
7. Mostly agree	17. Mostly agree
8. Mostly agree	18. Mostly agree
9. Mostly disagree	19. Mostly agree
10. Mostly agree	20. Mostly disagree

Step 4. Interpretation

Although the bureaucratic orientation scale is currently a self-examination and research tool, a very high score (15 or over) would suggest that you would enjoy working in a bureaucracy. A very low score (5 or lower) would suggest that you would be frustrated by working in a bureaucracy, especially a large one.

Step 5. How About Your College?

Do you think your score is representative of most college students in your major? Of most students at this university? Of most people who graduated from high school during the time when you did?

* Andrew J. Dubrin. *Human Relations: A Job Oriented Approach*, 1992, pp. 434-435. Reprinted by permission of Prentice Hall, Englewood Cliffs, New Jersey.

Exercise 14

You'll Play the Role, So Why Not Pick the Part?*

I. Purpose

(1) To help reinforce an understanding of the practical distinctions among the five organizational parts as defined by Mintzberg; and (2) to learn about the stereotypical perceptions that people hold about others who work in different functional areas of the company.

II. Group Size

The entire class will be divided, as discussed under step 3, into five groups.

III. Time Required

35 minutes broken down as follows: 5 minutes for group formation and project instructions; 20 minutes for group discussion; 10 minutes for reporting.

IV. **Preparation Required**

None except, perhaps, for advance reading of selections from Mintzberg's *Structure in Fives* (see excerpts at the end of this exercise).

V. **Materials**

None.

PROCESS

Step 1. Introduction

Thoroughly familiarize yourself with the five organizational parts identified by Mintzberg (*Structure in Fives*, 2nd ed., Englewood Cliffs, NJ: Prentice Hall, 1993). A brief statement from Mintzberg's ideas is provided at the end of this exercise.

Step 2. Your Preference

Rank the five organizational parts in *decreasing* order of your own *personal* preference for a major portion of your occupational career (i.e., #1=highest preference, #5=lowest preference) and, on the lines provided, write a one-sentence explanation for the ranking.

1. _____

_____

_____

_____

_____.

2. _____

_____

_____

_____

_____.

3. _____

_____

_____

_____

_____.

4. _____

_____

_____

_____

_____.

5. _____

_____

_____

_____

_____.

Step 3. Group Formation

Based on your responses to the above questions, or other criteria, as directed by your instructor, you will be assigned to one of five types of groups. The groups may be equal in size or they may be quite unequal in size. Regardless, each of the groups will correspond to one of the five organizational parts as defined by Mintzberg. Your group will be located in an area of the classroom that is spatially separated from the others in a manner corresponding to Mintzberg's logo (or "figure;" see Figures 1 and 2). That is, the Apex group should be located near the front of the classroom, the core in the back of the classroom and the midline centered between the two; the technostructure and support staff groups should be located on the extreme right and left sides of the room, respectively.

Step 4. Group Discussion

Although the exact assignment to the group will differ depending on the objectives of the course, the basic idea is to record (a) how you believe *you* would perceive *your* own organizational part and (b) as a member of this organizational part, how you believe you would perceive the other four organizational parts. Depending on your instructor's goals, these perceptions may focus on positive or negative attributes, cooperative or conflicting, or calculative political or another focuses.

Step 5. Group Report

Select one of your group members to report the conclusion of your discussion. A very brief statement (1–5 words) should suffice for each one of the five perceptions. Note: Past *experience* suggests that there may be derisive reactions to your statements (especially between staff and line units and between the apex and *all* other units), but *theory* suggests that all functions are necessary, so pay little attention to detractors!

Step 6. Class Discussion

Depending on the objectives of the course, this exercise will point out different principles. Nevertheless, on the basis of your experience in this exercise, how difficult do you believe it would it be for people in different functional areas of a company to form inaccurate stereotypes of one another? How can these stereotypes by avoided? What specific concepts in Mintzberg's organizational theory would be important in implementing these ideas? What other theories are relevant in this situation? Does TQM (Total Quality Management), for example, relate to these issues? Is organizational culture an important consideration? How relevant is personality in these concerns?

SELECTIONS FROM
STRUCTURE IN FIVES: DESIGNING EFFECTIVE ORGANIZATIONS,
BY HENRY MINTZBERG

The word *staff* should also be put into. . . [the organizational] context. In the early literature, the term was used in contrast to *line*; in principle, line positions had formal authority to make decisions, staff positions did not; they merely advised those who did. . . . This distinction between line and staff holds up in some kinds of structures (at least for the analytic staff, not the support staff) and breaks down in others.

Nevertheless, the distinction between line and staff is of some use to us, and we shall retain the terms here though in somewhat modified form. *Staff* will be used to refer to the technostructure *and* the support staff, those groups shown on either side of our theme diagram. *Line* will refer to the central part of the diagram, those managers in the flow of formal authority from the strategic apex to the operating core. Note that this definition does not mention the power to decide or advise. As we shall see, the support staff does not primarily advise; it has distinct functions to perform and decisions to make, although these relate only indirectly to the functions of the operating core. . . . Hence, while our logo shows the middle line as flaring out toward the bottom, it depicts both the technostructure and the support staff as forming ellipses. Later we shall see that, in fact, the specific shape varies according to the type of structure used by the organization.

Organizations have always had operators and top managers, people to do the basic work and people to hold the whole system together. As they grew, typically they first elaborated their middle-line component, to effect coordination by direct supervision. But as standardization became an accepted coordinating mechanism, the technostructure began to emerge. The work of Frederick Taylor gave rise to the "scientific management" movement of the 1920s, which saw the hiring of many work-study analysts. Just after World War II, the establishment of operations research and the advent of the computer pushed the influence of the technostructure well into the middle levels of many organizations.

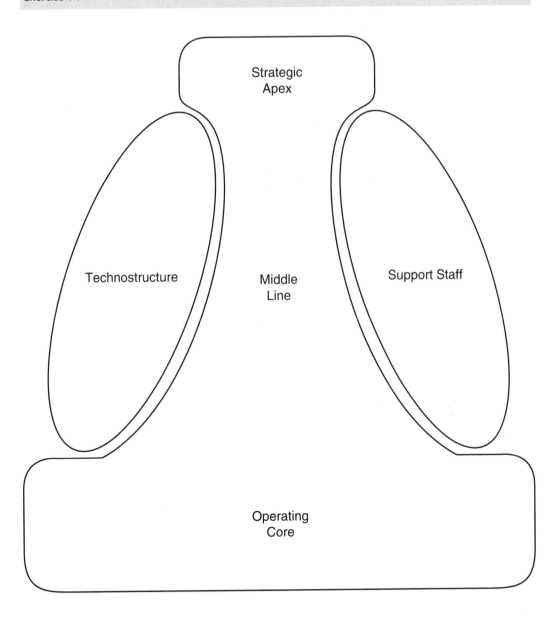

FIGURE 1 THE FIVE BASIC PARTS OF THE ORGANIZATION

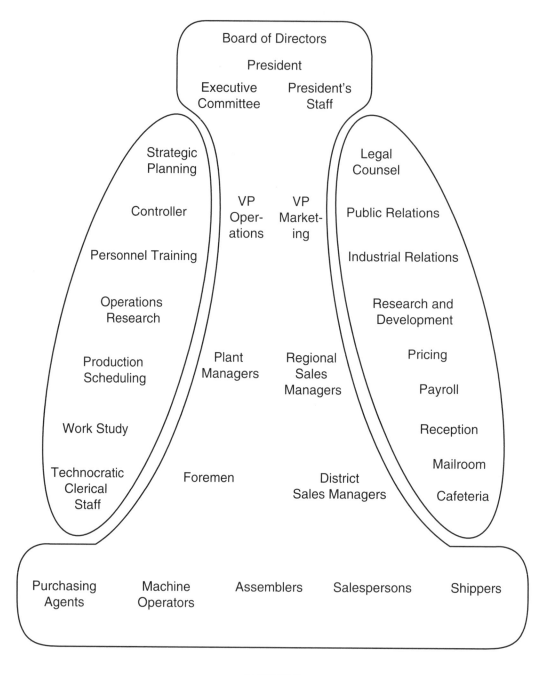

FIGURE 2
SOME MEMBERS AND UNITS OF THE MANUFACTURING FIRM

* Henry Mintzberg. *Structure in Fives: Designing Effective Organizations*, 1993, pp. 11, 18. Reprinted by permission of Prentice Hall, Englewood Cliffs, New Jersey.

Exercise 15

Designing Organizations For Art*

I. Purpose

To illustrate how uncertainty affects organizational design strategies. More specifically, the exercise draws on Galbraith's (1977) work to suggest that (a) characteristics of tasks, environment, and people affect uncertainty, and consequently, information-processing requirements; and (b) the varied strategies for dealing with uncertainty either reduce information-processing needs or enhance processing capabilities.

II. Group Size

Teams of 10 to 13 members each.

III. Time Required

1 1/2 to 2 hours.

IV. Preparation Required

Statement of client characteristics; background reading on organization design.

V. Materials

Poster material and a variety of art supplies (e.g., various colors of poster paper, scissors, Magic Markers, rulers).

PROCESS

Step 1. Introduction

As assigned by the instructor, read selected parts of Galbraith's *Organizational Design* or a similar work on principles of organizational design.

Step 2. Group Formation and Exercise Scenario

Your group is a newly formed advertising agency that specializes in the development of posters. Your agency has been contacted by a person or organization (your instructor will provide these details in a separate communication) and asked to propose a poster to meet the particular client's advertising needs. The following are the client's product specifications ("specs"):

1. At least three colors must appear on the poster.

2. The poster must contain some artwork/drawings.

3. A hard-hitting phrase or jingle that catches people's attention and stays with them must be part of the poster.

Your agency is in competition with several other poster agencies for this business, and your proposed poster must be ready for evaluation shortly.

The first task of your poster project team members is to deal with the issue of how they will organize themselves to produce the poster. You have hired a consultant who specializes in the application of organizational theory to operational problems. The consultant's recommendations are as follows:

1. The organization should be divided into three subgroups specializing in (a) layout (selection of poster's size, shape, colors, and general arrangement), (b) artwork, and (c) copy or written materials.

2. The subgroups should be physically separated to reduce unnecessary interaction. This should minimize confusion as to roles and responsibilities.

3. Coordination should occur through a hierarchy composed of subgroup leaders and a team leader.

Step 3. Organizational Design Planning

Your agency will have approximately 30 to 45 minutes to consider how you will organize yourselves to produce the proposed poster. You must react to the consultant's recommendations in your discussion and *submit a plan for organizing to the instructor*. This can be in the form of an organizational chart or a written statement.

Step 4. Production

Your agency will be supplied with a variety of art supplies and given approximately 1 hour to produce a poster.

Step 5. Presentation of the Product to the Client

Display of the poster and a brief description of its merits are to be given by the project team leader; questions from the client (i.e., the instructor and other class members) should be answered by other team members whose functions on the team are being addressed by the questions.

Step 6. Class Discussion about the Exercise

Some of the organizational design issues that may have been relevant to the functioning of your project team include the following:

1. Factors that contribute to task uncertainty.

2. Implications of uncertainty for coordination.

3. Trade-offs between specialization and coordination.

4. Implications of time pressure or task urgency on organizational design.

---

* Adapted from French, J.L. (1993). Simulating Organizational Design Issue. *Journal of Management Education*, 17(1), pp. 110-113.

6

CHANGE

Exercise 16

Dynamics of Change: Precipitated Resistance To Change in the Classroom*

I. Purpose

To demonstrate the various forms of resistance to change that may occur in an organizational setting.

II. Group Size

Individually, with small group discussion following.

III. Time Required

10 minutes for the exercise; 20 minutes for small group discussion.

IV. Preparation Required

None.

V. Materials

None.

PROCESS

Step 1. Precipitated Change

Your instructor will provide additional information for you to respond to, both individually and in small groups.

Step 2. Forms of Resistance

Categorize the responses to the instructor-provided information using the following list:

1. *Parochial self-interest*—a perception on the part of the individual that the change will cause him or her to personally lose something of value. The resistance reflects the person's attempt to protect his or her own personal goals (i.e., power, money, prestige, convenience, security, professional competence).

2. *Different assessments*—organizational members' level of resistance to change is directly affected by their individual perception and evaluation of the costs or benefits associated with the change.

3. *Low tolerance for change*—this factor relates directly to individual differences in ability to cope with change. Personal anxiety levels affect the individual tolerance for accepting change of any magnitude.

4. *Lack of understanding and trust*—this form of resistance may occur where the individual is either unclear about the intended purpose of the change or lacks a basic trust in the originator of the change.

Step 3. Discussion

Discuss the implications of varied degrees of resistance to change for the organization in small groups. Address specific techniques that may be useful in reducing the impact of resistance to change.

---

* Adapted from H. E. Baker, III, (1988). Dynamics of Change: Precipitated Resistance to Change in the Classroom. *Organizational Behavior Teaching Review*, 13(4), pp. 134-137.

Exercise 17

A Force-Field Analysis Of Student Government Participation*

I. Purpose

To apply Lewin's force field analysis model to the problem of student noninvolvement in university student government.

II. Group Size

Individually and in groups of 5 to 7 members each.

III. Time Required

40 to 45 minutes.

IV. Preparation Required

Read the Introduction section.

V. Materials

None.

PROCESS

Step 1. Introduction

A force-field analysis is one way to assess what is happening in an organization. This concept reflects the forces, driving and restraining, at work at a particular time. It helps to assess organizational strengths and to select forces to add or remove in order to create change. The theory of change suggested by Kurt Lewin, who developed the force-field analysis, is that while driving forces may be more easily affected, shifting them could increase opposition (tension and/or conflict) within the organization and add restraining forces. Therefore, it may be more effective to remove restraining forces to create change.

The use of the force-field analysis will demonstrate the range of forces pressing on an organization at a particular time. This analysis can increase the organization's optimism that it is possible to strategize and plan for change.

Step 2. Problem Analysis

Complete the Problem Analysis Section on pages 74 and 75.

Step 3. Force-Field Analysis

Put the driving and restraining forces of the problem on the force-field analysis form on page 76 according to their degree of impact on change.

Step 4. Group Discussion

In groups of 5 to 7, discuss the driving and restraining forces in each person's problem definition.

Step 5. Class Discussion

1. Why is it useful to break a problem situation up into driving and restraining forces?

2. Would the model be used any differently whether applied to an individual or organizational problem?

Problem Analysis Section

1. Describe the problem of student participation in university student government in a few words.

_____

_____

_____

_____

_____

_____

_____

_____

_____

_____

_____

_____

_____

2. A list of forces *driving* toward change would include:

    a. _____

    b. _____

    c. _____

    d. _____

    e. _____

    f. _____

3. A list of forces *restraining* change would include:

    a. _____

    b. _____

    c. _____

    d. _____

    e. _____

    f. _____

FORCE-FIELD ANALYSIS FORM

Driving Forces	Restraining Forces

....➤ ◄..

Low extreme
try to avoid

High extreme
try to attain

**Present
Balance Point**

* Reprinted by permission from pages 259-261 of *Organization Behavior Exercises and Cases*, by D. M. Hai; Copyright © 1986 by West Publishing Company. All rights reserved.

Exercise 18

Understanding Resistance To Change: The Jefferson Company*

I. **Purpose**

To demonstrate diverse responses to change.

II. **Group Size**

4 to 5 members per group.

III. **Time Required**

1 hour.

IV. **Preparation Required**

Adequate copies of confidential role information should be prepared in advance of class meeting.

V. **Materials**

None.

PROCESS

Step 1. Introduction

Each student reads the general information for the exercise. The class and instructor should read the general information together, in case there are any questions concerning the specifics of the exercise.

Step 2. Review of Key Issues

This old-line company with new partners needs to implement many changes. It needs to change its technology, its equipment, and its operating procedures, all of which will mean changes for Jefferson's employees and managers. These employees and managers have very different backgrounds and hence different perspectives about the firm.

The Jefferson Company is also facing a challenging competitive situation: Jefferson lags behind its many competitors (most with more resources) in technology, and the entire industry is confronted with shrinking profit margins. Furthermore, the new equipment needed is very expensive and will require substantial start-up time for employee training. The fact that the company was purchased in a leveraged buy out transaction means it is in a precarious debt position, with limited funds available to purchase new equipment. It must control its costs and generate enough cash to repay its high debt. Finally, Jefferson is a union shop, with preexisting labor-management contracts constraining its activities.

Step 3. Role Play

Each group will meet in an assigned area to complete the role-play portion of the exercise.

Step 4. Group Review

The next step is for the students to share the different outcomes from group meetings. Use the following questions to guide and structure your group's experience:

1. Did your group reach agreement about whether to purchase the new equipment? What was your decision?

2. Briefly describe the decision-making process in your group. Was your decision unanimous? If not, what coalitions were formed?

3. Were there any factors that helped or hindered your group's ability to decide about implementing the changes?

4. What factors *internal* to the Jefferson Company helped or hindered the change effort? What factors *external* to the company helped or hindered the change effort?

5. What are the advantages and disadvantages of different methods of overcoming resistance to change? In the short run? The long run?

6. Can anything be done if people refuse to adapt to a change situation?

GENERAL INFORMATION FOR ALL PARTICIPANTS

The Jefferson Company is a small printing company located in a large midwestern city. The company is engaged in the business of typesetting and offset printing, serving primarily large companies such as department stores and advertising agencies. Raymond Goss founded the Jefferson Company in 1930, and he managed the firm as sole stockholder for nearly 60 years. During that time, the company grew from a two-man shop to its present 28 employees. The firm's profit and loss statement showed earnings of $275,000 last year, on sales of $2.5 million. The Jefferson Company's competitors range from similar small printing shops to large divisions of Fortune 500 corporations.

Two months ago, at the age of 86, Raymond Goss sold the Jefferson Company in a leveraged buyout transaction. The purchaser was Joe Ryan, who is 35 years old with an MBA in finance. He is the Jefferson Company's new chief executive officer (CEO). Although Ryan has a background in administration, he has no experience with the printing industry.

The Jefferson Company operates in an industry that has experienced a number of substantial changes in recent years. First, the printing industry has undergone a high degree of technological change over the past decade. New printing equipment is both sophisticated and expensive: A typical machine may cost over $1 million. This new high-tech printing equipment requires the shop technicians to learn new complex operating procedures. Access to the training programs for learning these new skills is controlled by union rules, and is generally awarded on the basis of seniority. In addition, the printing industry's market structure has shifted. Competition has increased, and printers have been confronted with rising costs but falling prices, leading to rapidly shrinking margins.

Although Ryan has spent time at the Jefferson Company since the buyout, this week marks the beginning of his full-time involvement in the firm's operations. Ryan has just called a meeting in his office involving the following key staff: Lynne Porter, sales manager; Jack Bensen, shop foreman; and Dave Lewis, skilled technician and union steward. Lynne and Jack have been asked to attend because of their important roles in the company's sales and shop operations. Dave has been included because of his technical expertise as well as his position as the shop employees' union representative. The purpose of this meeting is to discuss the purchase of $750,000 worth of computerized equipment that Ryan saw at a printing industry trade show.

---

* Adapted from Reilly, A. H. (1992). Understanding resistance to change: The Jefferson Company exercise. *Journal of Management Education.* 16(3), 314-326. Sage Publications, Inc.

EFFECTIVENESS

Exercise 19

When Is a Business Effective in the United States . . . and in Australia, India, Japan, and Korea?*

I. Purpose

To learn about an eight-level hierarchy of goals that U.S. corporate executives hold for business enterprises and to compare such rankings with those of businesspeople in several different nations.

II. Group Size

Individually or through consensus in groups of 4 to 7 members each.

III. Time Required

10 to 30 minutes, depending on group sizes and overall class membership.

IV. Preparation Required

None.

V. Materials

None.

PROCESS

Step 1. Rank Order of Goals of Business Executives

In a series of cross-cultural studies, George W. England asked business executives to assess the relative importance of eight goals that are often mentioned as basic to business activity. Based on your general knowledge and intuition, place the numbers 1 through 8 in each column of Form A to indicate your opinion of the relative importance of the goals in the countries indicated; let 1=most important and 8=least important. Although some goals may seem more similar than others, for the purpose of this exercise use only whole numbers and each number only once to indicate the rank order.

Step 2. Time Relevance and/or Group Consensus

Based on the objectives for the course, your instructor may ask you to fill in Form B with somewhat different instructions than those of step 1.

BUSINESS GOALS IN FIVE COUNTRIES — FORM A

Business Goals	*Australia*	*India*	*Japan*	*Korea*	*U.S.A.*
High productivity					
Industry leadership					
Employee welfare					
Organizational stability					
Profit maximization					
Organizational efficiency					
Social welfare					
Organizational growth					

BUSINESS GOALS IN FIVE COUNTRIES — FORM B

Business Goals	Australia	India	Japan	Korea	U.S.A.
High productivity					
Industry leadership					
Employee welfare					
Organizational stability					
Profit maximization					
Organizational efficiency					
Social welfare					
Organizational growth					

---

* Adapted from England, George W., O. P. Dhingra, and Naresh C. Agarwal. *The Manager and the Man: A Cross-Cultural Study of Personal Values.* Kent, Ohio: Kent State University Press, 1974, pp. 29-32.

Campus Organizational Assessment*

I. Purpose

One of the more popular approaches to measuring organizational effectiveness is Organizational Assessment (O.A.), a branch of the field of Organizational Development (O.D.). The purpose of this exercise is to apply, and develop an interpretation of, a widely used O.A. instrument.

II. Group Size

Any number of groups of 3 to 5 members each.

III. Time Required

50 to 150 minutes.

IV. Preparation Required

None.

V. Materials

None.

PROCESS

Step 1. Introduction

One of the first steps in organization development is doing an organizational assessment to evaluate the strengths and weaknesses of the organization. You and your team have been hired as a consulting group by the university to assess the strengths and weaknesses of the university. You are to collect data from your group members in these five areas:

1. Academics and scholarly environment

2. Quality of teaching on campus

3. Campus social life

4. Cultural events on campus

5. Management by the university administration

After you have gathered the data, evaluate the strengths and weaknesses and make recommendations for intervention. These recommendations must be very specific so that the university administration could implement them tomorrow without any more explanation. Avoid saying things like, "Teachers need to lecture better." Be specific by saying things such as, "We found 10% of the teachers didn't talk loud enough in class" or "50% of teachers get off the subject too frequently."

Step 2. Campus Profile and Assessment

	Not true	*1*	*2*	*3*	*4*	*5*	*Very true*

I. <u>Academics</u>

1 2 3 4 5	1. There is a wide range of courses to choose from.
1 2 3 4 5	2. Classroom standards are too easy.
1 2 3 4 5	3. The library is adequate.
1 2 3 4 5	4. Textbooks are helpful.

II. <u>Teachers</u>

    1 2 3 4 5   1. Teachers are committed to quality instruction.

    1 2 3 4 5   2. We have a high quality faculty.

    1 2 3 4 5   3. Teachers have a good balance between theory and practice.

III. <u>Social</u>

    1 2 3 4 5   1. Students are friendly to one another.

    1 2 3 4 5   3. It's difficult to make friends.

    1 2 3 4 5   4. Faculty gets involved in student activities.

    1 2 3 4 5   5. Too much energy goes into drinking and goofing off.

IV. <u>Cultural Events</u>

    1 2 3 4 5   1. There are ample activities on campus.

    1 2 3 4 5   2. Student activities are boring.

    1 2 3 4 5   3. The administration places a high value on student activities.

    1 2 3 4 5   4. Too much emphasis is placed on sports.

    1 2 3 4 5   5. We need more "cultural" activities.

V. <u>Organizational Management</u>

    1 2 3 4 5   1. Decision making is shared at all levels of the organization.

    1 2 3 4 5   2. There is unity and cohesiveness between departments and units.

    1 2 3 4 5   3 Too many departmental clashes hamper the organization's effectiveness.

    1 2 3 4 5   4. Students have a say in many decisions.

    1 2 3 4 5   5. The budgeting process seems fair.

    1 2 3 4 5   6. Recruiting and staffing are handled thoughtfully with student needs in mind.

Step 3. Identify Organization's Strengths

1. In academics _____

_____

2. In teaching _____

_____

3. In social life _____

_____

4. In cultural activities _____

_____

5. In management _____

_____

Step 4. Identify Organization's Weaknesses

1. In academics _____

_____

2. In teaching _____

_____

3. In social life _____

_____

4. In cultural activities _____

_____

5. In management _____

_____

Step 5. Identify Interventions

What interventions would you recommend to resolve weaknesses and build on strengths?

1. In academics

   A. _____

   _____

   B. _____

   _____

2. In teaching

   A. _____

   _____

   B. _____

   _____

3. In social life

   A. _____

   _____

   B. _____

   _____

4. In cultural activities

   A. _____

   _____

   B. _____

   _____

5. In management

   A. _____

   _____

   B. _____

   _____

Step 6. Executive Summary of the Report

Write an executive summary of your report, giving an introduction and statement of purpose. Then do a summary of your major findings and your recommendations. Remember to be specific. Executive summaries need to say as much as possible with a minimum of words, using the English language efficiently.

_____

_____

_____

_____

_____

_____

_____

_____

_____

_____

_____

_____

_____

* Adapted from Marcic, D. (1990). Organizational assessment of campus. *Organizational Behavior: Experiences and Cases*. St.Paul, MN: West Publishing Company, pp. 326-329.

Exercise 21

Fast Food and Effectiveness: An Organizational Diagnosis Exercise*

I. Purpose

(1) To diagnose an organization in terms of goals, policies, procedures, structure, climate, technology, environment, job design, communication, and leadership; and (2) to compare and contrast two organizations on these variables.

II. Group Size

Subgroups of 4 to 6 members each.

III. Time Required

Several days' out-of-class preparation; 50 minutes or 1 hour in class, depending on size of total group.

IV. Preparation Required

Form groups and do steps 1 and 2 in advance. Be prepared to report your diagnosis and recommendations to management to the rest of the class on the assigned day.

V. Materials

None.

PROCESS

Step 1. Introduction

A critical first step in improving or changing any organization is *diagnosing*, or analyzing, its present functioning. Many change and organization development efforts fall short of their objectives because this important step was not taken or was conducted superficially. Imagine how you would feel if you went to your doctor complaining of stomach pains, and the doctor recommended surgery without conducting any tests, without obtaining any further information, and without a careful physical examination. You would probably switch doctors! Yet managers often attempt major changes with correspondingly little diagnostic work in advance. In this exercise you are asked to conduct a group diagnosis of two different organizations in the fast-food business. The exercise provides an opportunity to integrate much of the knowledge you have gained in other exercises and in studying other topics. Your task is to describe the organizations as carefully as you can in terms of several key organizational concepts. Although the organizations are probably very familiar to you, try to step back and look at them as though you were seeing them for the first time.

Step 2. Your Assignment

The group will be formed into subgroups of four or six people. Your assignment is described as follows:

One experience most people in the United States have shared is that of dining in the hamburger establishment known as McDonald's. In fact, someone has claimed that twenty-fifth-century archaeologists may dig into the ruins of our present civilization and conclude that twentieth-century religion was devoted to the worship of golden arches.

Your group, Fastalk Consultants, is known as the shrewdest but most insightful management consulting firm in the country. You have been hired by Bhik Maak, McDonald's president, to make recommendations for improving the motivation and performance of personnel in their franchise operations. Let us assume that key job activities in franchise operations are food preparation, order taking and dealing with customers, and routine clean-up operations.

Recently Maak has come to suspect that his company's competitors such as Burger King, Wendy's, Jack in the Box, various pizza establishments, and others are making heavy inroads into McDonald's market. He has also hired a market research firm to investigate and compare the relative merits of the sandwiches, french fries, and drinks served in McDonald's and those in one of the competitors, and has asked the market research firm to assess the advertising campaigns of the two organizations. Hence, you will not need to be concerned with marketing issues, except as they may have an impact on employee behavior. The president wants *you* to look into the *organization* of the franchises to determine the strengths and weaknesses of each. Select a competitor that gives McDonald's a good run for its money in your area.

Maak has established an unusual contract with you: He wants you to make your recommendations based on your observations *as a customer*. He does not want you to do a complete diagnosis with interviews, surveys, or behind-the-scenes observations. He wants your report in two parts.

1. Given his organization's goals of profitability, sales volume, fast and courteous service, and cleanliness, he wants an analysis that will compare and contrast McDonald's and the competitor in terms of the following concepts:

   Organizational goals
   Organizational structure
   Technology
   Environment
   Employee motivation
   Communication
   Leadership style
   Policies procedures/rules/standards
   Job design
   Organizational climate

2. Given the corporate goals listed under part 1, what specific actions might McDonald's management and franchise owners take in the following areas to achieve these goals (profitability, sales volume, fast and courteous service, and cleanliness)?

   Job design and workflow
   Organization structure (at the individual restaurant level)
   Employee incentives
   Leadership
   Employee selection

Step 3. Initial Assessment

How do McDonald's and the competitor differ in these aspects? Which company has the better approach?

Step 4. Some Guidelines

1. Substantiate your recommendations by referring to one or more theories of motivation, leadership, small groups, or job design.

2. The president wants concrete, specific, and practical recommendations. Avoid vague generalizations such as "improve communications" or "increase trust." Say very clearly *how* management can improve organizational performance.

3. As you make your group presentation, the rest of the group will play the role of the top management executive committee. They may be a bit skeptical. They will ask tough questions. They will have to be sold on your ideas.

4. You will have 10 minutes in which to present your ideas to the executive committee and to respond to their questions.

Step 5. 3-Hour-Outside-of-Class Preparation

Complete the assignment by going as a group to one McDonald's and one competitor's restaurant. If possible, have a meal in each place. To get a more valid comparison, visit a McDonald's and a competitor located in the same area. After observing each restaurant, meet with your group and prepare your 10-minute report to the executive committee.

Step 6. Class Report

In class, each subgroup will present its report to the rest of the group, who will act as the executive committee. The group leader will appoint a timekeeper to be sure that each subgroup sticks to its 10-minute time limit.

---

* Adapted from Lewicki, R. J., Bowan, D. D., Hall, D. T. & Hall, F. S. (1988). *Experience in Management and Organizational Behavior*. Organizational Diagnosis: Fast Food Technology, New York: John Wiley & Sons, pp. 224-227.

CULTURE

Exercise 22

Excellence on the College Campus*

I. Purpose

(1) To become familiar with the conclusions of the most widely read management book of the 1980s; (2) to apply the principles that underlie these conclusions to a familiar setting: the college campus; and (3) to critically examine the theory and the campus for possible improvements, in theory and in an actual organization.

II. Group Size

Unlimited.

III. Time Required

Approximately 20 minutes if participants have already read the material (provided at the end of this exercise).

IV. Preparation Required

Advance reading may be assigned.

V. Materials

None.

PROCESS

Step 1. Introduction

When assigned, read the selection (found at the end of this exercise) from Tom Peters and Robert Waterman's best-selling management book of the 1980s, *In Search of Excellence: Lessons from America's Best-Run Companies*, in which they report how they studied 43 excellent U.S. companies and looked for common themes. They found that a strong, dominant culture that is lived by top management is crucial to obtaining a truly high level of excellence.

Step 2. Application

Think about the college or university you are attending and answer the following questions:

1. What are the boundaries of the campus?

_____

_____

_____

_____

_____

2. Within these boundaries, how well do the eight characteristics that Peters and Waterman discuss describe the campus? On table on page 98, check the column for each of the eight characteristics which best describes your opinion of the campus.

	Strongly Agree	Somewhat Agree	Not Sure	Somewhat Disagree	Strongly Disagree
	1	*2*	*3*	*4*	*5*
1. A bias for action					
2. Close to the customer					
3. Autonomy and entrepreneurship					
4. Productivity through people					
5. Hands-on, value driven					
6. Stick to the knitting					
7. Simple form, lean staff					
8. Simultaneous loose–tight properties					

Step 3. Analysis

Compare your answers with others in the class or discussion group. Are there differences? If there are differences, what is their source? What are the cultural strengths of the college? Are there areas where the college could improve its culture? What suggestions would you make to the college administration to bring about these improvements?

CHARACTERISTICS OF EXCELLENT COMPANIES

1. **A bias for action.** A bias for action, for getting on with it. Even though these companies may be analytical in their approach to decision making, they are not paralyzed by the fact (as so many others seem to be). In many of these companies the standard operating procedure is "Do it, fix it, try it." Says a Digital Equipment Corporation senior executive, for example, "When we've got a big problem here, we grab ten senior guys and stick them in a room for a week. They come

up with an answer and implement it." Moreover, the companies are experimenters supreme. Instead of allowing 250 engineers and marketers to work on a new product in isolation for fifteen months, they form bands of 5 to 25 and test ideas out on a customer, often with inexpensive prototypes, within a matter of weeks. What is striking is the host of practical devices the excellent companies employ, to maintain corporate fleetness of foot and counter the stultification that almost inevitably comes with size.

2. **Close to the customer.** These companies learn from the people they serve. They provide unparalleled quality, service, and reliability—things that work and last. They succeed in differentiating—*a la* Frito-Lay (potato chips), Maytag (washers), or Tupperware—the most commodity-like products. IBM's marketing vice president, Francis G. (Buck) Rodgers, says, "It's a shame that, in so many companies, whenever you get good service, it's an exception." Not so at the excellent companies. Everyone gets into the act. Many of the innovative companies got their best product ideas from customers. That comes from listening, intently and regularly.

3. **Autonomy and entrepreneurship.** The innovative companies foster many leaders and many innovators throughout the organization. They are a hive of what we've come to call champions; 3M has been described as "so intent on innovation that its essential atmosphere seems not like that of a large corporation but rather a loose network of laboratories and cubbyholes populated by feverish inventors and dauntless entrepreneurs who let their imaginations fly in all directions." They don't try to hold everyone on so short a rein that he can't be creative. They encourage practical risk taking, and support good tries. They follow Fletcher Byrom's ninth commandment: "Make sure you generate a reasonable number of mistakes."

4. **Productivity through people.** The excellent companies treat the rank and file as the root source of quality and productivity gain. They do not foster we/they labor attitudes or regard capital investment as the fundamental source of efficiency improvement. As Thomas J. Watson, Jr., said of his company, "IBM's philosophy is largely contained in three simple beliefs. I want to begin with what I think is the most important: *our respect for the individual*. This is a simple concept, but in IBM it occupies a major portion of management time." Texas Instrument's chairman Mark Shepherd talks about it in terms of every worker being "seen as a source of ideas, not just acting as a pair of hands"; each of his more than *9,000* People Involvement Program, or

PIP, teams (TI's quality circles) does contribute to the company's sparkling productivity record.

5. **Hands-on, value driven.** Thomas Watson, Jr., said that "the basic philosophy of an organization has far more to do with its achievements than do technological or economic resources, organizational structure, innovation and timing." Watson and HP's William Hewlett are legendary for walking the plant floors. McDonalds Ray Kroc regularly visits stores and assesses them on the factors the company holds dear, Q.S.C. & V. (Quality, Service, Cleanliness, and Value).

6. **Stick to the knitting.** Robert W. Johnson, former Johnson & Johnson chairman, put it this way: "Never acquire a business you don't know how to run." Or as Edward G. Harness, past chief executive at Proctor & Gamble, said, "This company has never left its base. We seek to be anything but a conglomerate." While there were a few exceptions, the odds for excellent performance seem strongly to favor those companies that stay reasonably close to businesses they know.

7. **Simple form, lean staff.** As big as most of the companies we have looked at are, none when we looked at it was formally run with a matrix organization structure, and some which had tried that form had abandoned it. The underlying structural forms and systems in the excellent companies are elegantly simple. Top-level staffs are lean; it is not uncommon to find a corporate staff of fewer than 100 people running multibillion-dollar enterprises.

8. **Simultaneous loose-tight properties.** The excellent companies are both centralized and decentralized. For the most part, as we have said, they have pushed autonomy down to the shop floor or product development team. On the other hand, they are fanatic centralists around the few core values they hold dear. 3M is marked by barely organized chaos surrounding its product champions. Yet one analyst argues, "The brainwashed members of an extremist political sect are no more conformist in their central beliefs." At Digital the chaos is so rampant that one executive noted, "Damn few people know who they work for." Yet Digital's fetish for reliability is more rigidly adhered to than any outsider could imagine.

---

* Selected excerpt from pages 13-16 of *In Search of Excellence* by T. J. Peters and R.H. Waterman, Jr. Copyright © 1982 by Thomas J. Peters and Robert H. Waterman, Jr. Reprinted by permission of HarperCollins Publishers, Inc.

Exercise 23

A Culture in the Forest*

I. Purpose

To become familiar with the basic components of organizational culture by considering an unusual "nonprofit" organizational setting.

II. Group Size

Individually or in groups of 5 to 7 members each.

III. Time Required

15 to 30 minutes.

IV. Preparation Required

None, other than reading the very brief case, if assigned, prior to the class.

V. Materials

None.

PROCESS

Step 1. Introduction

When assigned by the instructor, read the following case of an organization that is widely known although not exactly well documented!

A YOUNG ENTREPRENEUR

It was early in the spring of the second year of his insurrection against the High Sheriff of Nottingham that Robin Hood took a walk in Sherwood Forest. As he walked, he pondered the progress of the campaign, the disposition of his forces, his opposition's moves, and the options that confronted him.

The revolt against the Sheriff began as a personal crusade. It erupted out of Robin's own conflict with the Sheriff and his administration. Alone, however, he could accomplish little. He therefore sought allies, men with personal grievances and a deep sense of justice. Later he took all who came without asking too many questions. Strength, he believed, lay in numbers.

The first year was spent in forging the group into a disciplined band—a group united in enmity against the Sheriff, willing to live outside the law as long as it took to accomplish their goals. The band was simply organized. Robin ruled supreme, making all important decisions. Specific tasks were delegated to his lieutenants. Will Scarlett was in charge of intelligence and scouting. His main job was to keep tabs on the movements of the Sheriff's men. He also collected information on the travel plans of rich merchants and abbots. Little John kept discipline among the men, and saw to it that their archery was at the high peak that their profession demanded. Scarlock took care of the finances, paying shares of the take, bribing officials, converting loot to cash, and finding suitable hiding places for surplus gains. Finally, Much the Miller's Son had the difficult task of provisioning the ever increasing band.

The increasing size of the band was a source of satisfaction for Robin but also of much concern. The fame of his Merrymen was spreading, and new recruits were pouring in. Yet the number of men was beginning to exceed the food capacity of the forest. Game was becoming scarce, and food had to be transported by cart from outlying villages. The band had always camped together. But now what had been a small gathering had become a major encampment that could be detected miles away. Discipline was also becoming harder to enforce. "Why!" Robin reflected, "I don't know half the men I run into these days."

While the band was getting larger, their main source of revenue was in decline. Travelers, especially the richer variety, began giving the forest a wide berth. This was costly and inconvenient to them, but it was preferable to having all their goods confiscated by Robin's men. Thus Robin was considering changing his past policy to one of a fixed transit tax.

The idea was strongly resisted by his lieutenants, who were proud of the Merrymen's famous motto: "Rob from the rich and give to the poor." The poor and the townspeople, they argued, were their main source of support and information. If they were antagonized by transit taxes they would abandon the Merrymen to the mercy of the Sheriff.

Robin wondered how long they could go on keeping to the ways and methods of their early days. The Sheriff was growing stronger. He had the money, the men, and the facilities. In the long run he would wear Robin and his men down. Sooner or later, he would find their weaknesses and methodically destroy them. Robin felt that he must bring the campaign to a conclusion. The question was how this could be achieved?

Robin knew that the chances of killing or capturing the Sheriff were remote. Besides, killing the Sheriff might satisfy his personal thirst for revenge, but would not change the basic problem. It was also unlikely that the Sheriff would be removed from office. He had powerful friends at court. On the other hand, Robin reflected, if the district was in a perpetual state of unrest, and the taxes went uncollected, the Sheriff would fall out of favor. But on further thought, Robin reasoned, the Sheriff might shrewdly use the unrest to obtain more reinforcements.

The outcome depended on the mood of the regent Prince John. The Prince was known as vicious, volatile and unpredictable. He was obsessed by his unpopularity among the people, who wanted the imprisoned King Richard back. He also lived in constant fear of the barons, who daily were growing more hostile to his power. Several of these barons had set out to collect the ransom that would release King Richard the Lionheart from his prison in Austria. Robin had been discreetly asked to join the barons, in return for future amnesty. It was a dangerous proposition. Provincial banditry was one thing, court intrigue another. Prince John was known for his vindictiveness. If the gamble failed he would personally see to it that all involved were crushed.

Step 2. Discussion

Discuss the following questions in small groups, or consider them individually, and be prepared to present your answers in class.

1. What are the central values of this culture, and what rituals, would you imagine, help to reinforce these values?

2. Who is the hero of the culture of this organization and what networks would be able to support the hero's status?

3. How strong is this culture? It the culture a dominant feature of the organization as reported? Is the culture "lived by top management"?

4. It would seem as if organizational size has become a major factor in the problems considered by Hood. How has organizational size affected the nature of this organization's culture?

5. Given the issues that Hood is pondering, do you envision any changes in the band's culture in the near future? Why or why not? If you do see changes, are envisioned, what might they be?

---

* Joseph Lampel, McGill University. Copyright © 1985. Reproduced by permission.

Exercise 24

Four Corporate Cultures*

I. Purpose

(1) To explore the effects of cultural behaviors or descriptions on others; (2) to experience cross-cultural encounters; and (3) to increase awareness of how cultural mannerisms and rituals are derived from cultural attitudes.

II. Group Size

Sets of 4 groups with 4 to 8 members each.

III. Time Required

30 minutes at a minimum, with 50 or 75 minutes being ideal.

IV. Preparation Required

Read assigned selections from Deal and Kennedy's *Corporate Culture: The Rites and Rituals of Corporate Life* (Addison-Wesley, 1982) or the excerpt presented at the end of this exercise.

V. Materials

Masking tape; small paperclips; raisins, peanuts, or small candy; group name signs for the "host" organization; a newsprint poster on which is printed the schedule of visits for the groups as follows:

Round 1:   Group 2 visits Group 1 and
               Group 4 visits Group 3.

Round 2:   Group 3 visits Group 2 and
               Group 1 visits Group 4.

Round 3:   Group 3 visits Group 1 and
               Group 4 visits Group 2.

PROCESS

Step 1. Introduction

The instructor introduces the exercise, and the participants are divided into four groups and assigned to different areas in the room or separate rooms, if available.

Step 2. Rehearsal

The instructor announces, PRIVATELY, to each group the cultural description it is to portray. The group plans and rehearses its assigned culture. The following is a fairly natural sequence of welcoming visitors. Your group is to create specific ways of expressing each activity in accordance with the descriptions and characteristics that are distinctive of your group. Be as verbal as you want to be and create as many gestures as you wish, but be careful that the *way* in which you express yourself reflects your cultural descriptions.

1. The equivalent of waving "hello" as guests approach from a distance.

2. The equivalent of a close greeting, such as the custom of shaking hands.

3. The equivalent of inviting your guests to come in or to come with you.

4. The equivalent of inviting your guests to sit down (on a chair, the floor, etc.).

5. The equivalent of seeing your guests to the door and bidding them farewell.

Step 3. More Instructions

When all groups have developed their strategies for portraying their assigned cultural description, the instructor calls time and gives each *host* group a paper cup full of raisins, peanuts, or small candy. The food will be the refreshments that the host group will have available to offer visitors. The instructor then directs the visiting group to find its assigned host (the host will have a sign indicating its coded group identification number).

Step 4. The Meeting

The instructor announces the beginning of Round 1, and the groups conduct their first visits according to the posted schedule. At the end of approximately 10 minutes, the instructor suggests that the visitors begin their farewells. At the end of 15 minutes, the instructor calls time and directs the members of each group to return to their area and to discuss among themselves their reactions to the activity. During this time, the instructor refills the paper cups.

Step 5. Silent Report

The groups then tell the instructor, *PRIVATELY,* which cultural description they believe the other group was attempting to portray.

Step 6. More Rounds

The instructor conducts Rounds 2 and 3 in the same manner as Round 1, allowing a few minutes for group discussion and refilling of the cups at the completion of each round.

Step 7. The Debriefing

The entire class is assembled, and the instructor leads a discussion of reactions to and perceptions resulting from the experience.

DESCRIPTIONS OF FOUR CULTURES

Now it is time to put all of these factors together—values, heroes, rites and rituals and see how they actually work within the corporation. The focus is on managing cultures—that is, on understanding them, analyzing them, shaping them, and retooling them when change is necessary. Most of the information here is suggestive, not prescriptive. We intend it as a different way of looking at management within an organization and we hope that it will offer a new perspective for both managers and employees. . . [T]he biggest single influence on a company's culture is the broader social and business environment in which the company operates. A corporate culture embodies what it takes to succeed in this environment. If hard selling is required for success, the culture will be one that encourages people to sell and sell hard; if thoughtful technical decision-making is required, the culture will make sure that that happens too.

After examining hundreds of corporation and their business environments, we have come to see that many companies fall into four general categories or types of cultures. These categories are determined by two factors in the marketplace: the degree of risk associated with the company's activities, and the speed at which companies—and their employees—get feedback on whether decisions or strategies are successful. From these market realities, we have distilled the four generic cultures:

The tough-guy, macho culture. A world of individualists who regularly take high risks and get quick feedback on whether their actions were right or wrong.

The work hard / play hard culture. Fun and action are the rule here, and employees take few risks, all with quick feedback; to succeed, the culture encourages them to maintain a high level of relatively low-risk activity.

The bet-your-company culture. Cultures with big-stakes decisions, where years pass before employees know whether decisions have paid off. A high-risk, slow-feedback environment.

The process culture. A world of little or no feedback where employees find it hard to measure what they do; instead they concentrate on how it's done. We have another name for this culture when the processes get out of control—bureaucracy!

The division of the world of business into four categories is, of course, simplistic. No company we know today precisely fits into any one of these categories. In fact, within any single real-world company, a mix of all four types of cultures will be found. Marketing department are tough-guy cultures. Sales and manufacturing departments work hard and play hard. Research and development is a world of high risk and slow feedback. And accounting sits squarely in the upper reaches of bureaucratic life.

Moreover, companies with very strong cultures—the companies that most intrigue us—fit this simple mold hardly at all. These companies have cultures that artfully blend the best elements of all four types—and blend them in ways that allow these companies to perform well when the environment around them changes, as it inevitably does. However, we do think that this framework can be useful in helping managers begin to identify more specifically the culture of their own companies.

* Reprinted from L. D. Goodstein and J. W, Pfeiffer (Eds.), *The 1993 Annual for Facilitators, Trainers, and Consultants.* San Diego, CA: Pfeiffer and Company, 1983. Used with permission. Pp. 107-108 from Terrance E. Deal and Allan A. Kennedy, *Corporate Cultures: The Rites and Rituals of Coporate Life.* © 1982 Addison-Wesley Publishing Company. Reprinted by permission.

CONFLICT

Exercise 25

Conflict Strategies*

I. Purpose

Different persons learn different ways of managing conflicts. The strategies you use to manage conflicts may be quite different from those used by your friends and acquaintances. This exercise gives you an opportunity to increase your awareness of what conflict strategies you use and how they compare with the strategies employed by others.

II. Group Size

4 to 6 individuals each.

III. Time Required

10 minutes to complete questionnaire; 20 minutes for group discussion.

IV. Preparation Required

None.

V. Materials

None.

PROCESS

Step 1. Form Groups

With your classmates, form groups of 4 to 6 members each.

Step 2. Complete Questionnaire

Working by yourself, complete the questionnaire titled "How You Act in Conflicts."

Step 3. Scoring Questionnaire

Score your questionnaire, using the scoring table that follows the questionnaire.

Step 4. Stengths and Weaknesses

Each group discusses the strengths and weaknesses of each of the conflict strategies provided by the instructor.

VARIATION

Step 1. Form Groups

Form groups of 6 members each. Make sure you know the other members of your group. Do not join a group of strangers.

Step 2. Complete Questionnaire

Working by yourself, complete the questionnaire.

Step 3. Conflict Strategies

Working by yourself, read the discussion of conflict strategies provided by the instructor. Then make five slips of paper. Write the names of the other five members of your group on the slips of paper, one name to a slip.

Step 4. Identify Strategy

On each slip of paper write the conflict strategy that best fits the actions of the person named.

Step 5. Compare Assessments

After all group members are finished, pass out your slips of paper to the persons whose names are on them. You all should end up with five slips of paper, each containing a description of your conflict style as seen by another group member.

Step 6. Scoring

Score your questionnaire, using the scoring table. Rank the five conflict strategies from the one you use the most to the one you use the least. This will give you an indication of how you see your own conflict strategy. The second most frequently used strategy is your backup strategy, the one you use if your first one fails.

Step 7. Describe Individual Strategy

After drawing names to see who goes first, one member describes the results of his or her own questionnaire. This is the member's view of his or her own conflict strategies. The member then reads each of the five slips of paper on which are written the views of the other group members about the member's conflict strategy. Next the member asks the other group members to give specific examples of how they have seen him or her act in conflicts. The group members should use the rules for constructive feedback. The person to the left of the first member repeats this procedure, and so on around the group.

Step 8. Strengths and Weaknesses

Each group discusses the strengths and weaknesses of each of the conflict strategies.

HOW YOU ACT IN CONFLICTS

Proverbs state traditional wisdom, and these proverbs reflect traditional wisdom for resolving conflicts. Read each of the proverbs carefully. Using the following scale, indicate how typical each proverb is of your actions in a conflict.

    5=very typical of the way I act in a conflict

    4=frequently typical of the way I act in a conflict

    3=sometimes typical of the way I act in a conflict

    2=seldom typical of the way I act in a conflict

    1=never typical of the way I act in a conflict

_4_   1. It is easier to refrain, than to retreat, from a quarrel.

_3_   2. If you cannot make a person think as you do, make him or her do as you think.

_3_   3. Soft words win hard hearts.

_2_   4. You scratch my back, I'll scratch yours.

_5_   5. Come now and let us reason together.

_4_   6. When two quarrel, the person who keeps silent first is the most praiseworthy.

_2_   7. Might overcomes right.

_3_   8. Smooth words make smooth ways.

_4_   9. Better half a loaf than no bread at all.

_3_   10. Truth lies in knowledge, not in majority opinion.

_1_   11. He who fights and runs away lives to fight another day.

_1_   12. He hath conquered well that hath made his enemies flee.

_2_   13. Kill your enemies with kindness.

_5_   14. A fair exchange brings no quarrel.

_4_   15. No person has the final answer, but every person has a piece to contribute.

_4_   16. Stay away from people who disagree with you.

_2_   17. Fields are won by those who believe in winning.

_4_   18. Kind words are worth much and cost little.

_1_   19. Tit for tat is fair play.

_3_   20. Only the person who is willing to give up his or her monopoly on truth can ever profit from the truths that others hold.

_3_   21. Avoid quarrelsome people as they will only make your life miserable.

_1_   22. A person who will not flee will make others flee.

_3_   23. Soft words ensure harmony.

_3_   24. One gift for another makes good friends.

_5_   25. Bring your conflicts into the open and face them directly; only then will the best solution be discovered.

_1_   26. The best way of handling conflicts is to avoid them.

_3_   27. Put your foot down where you mean to stand.

_3_   28. Gentleness will triumph over anger.

_4_   29. Getting part of what you want is better than not getting anything at all.

_4_   30. Frankness, honesty, and trust will move mountains.

_2_   31. There is nothing so important you have to fight for it.

_2_   32. There are two kinds of people in the world, the winners and the losers.

___2___   33. When one hits you with a stone, hit him or her with a piece of cotton.

___4___   34. When both give in halfway, a fair settlement is achieved.

___3___   35. By digging and digging, the truth is discovered.

SCORING TABLE				
Type I	*Type II*	*Type III*	*Type IV*	*Type V*
1. 4	2. 3	3. 3	4. 2	5. 5
6. 4	7. 2	8. 3	9. 4	10. 3
11. 1	12. 1	13. 2	14. 5	15. 4
16. 4	17. 2	18. 4	19. 1	20. 3
21. 3	22. 1	23. 3	24. 3	25. 5
26. 1	27. 3	28. 3	29. 4	30. 4
31. 2	32. 2	33. 2	34. 4	35. 3
Total 19	Total 14	Total 20	Total 23	Total 27

* Adapted from Johnson, D. W. & Johnson, F. P. (1982). Your Conflict Strategies
   Exercise. *Joining Together: Group Theory & Group Skills.* Englewood Cliffs,
   NJ: Prentice Hall, pp. 281-285.

Exercise 26

Interpersonal Communication/Conflict Role Plays*

I. Purpose

To practice different means of resolving interpersonal difficulties.

II. Group Size

Varies by role play.

III. Time Required

20 minutes for each of the first three role plays; 40 minutes for the fourth one.

IV. Preparation Required

None.

V. Materials

None.

INSTRUCTIONS: FOR ROLE PLAYS 1, 2, AND 3

Step 1. Introduction

Your instructor will provide three short role plays relating to interpersonal conflict and communication on the job. Your instructor may ask you to do one or more of them.

Step 2. Setup

1. Volunteers are selected for the following:

   a. One person to play subordinate role
   b. Two or three for the supervisor's role

2. All volunteers go into the hall and read only their own part. Meanwhile, the instructor briefs the class on the role play. Class members do not read at this time.

Step 3. Role Plays

The subordinate and one supervisor come in to play the situation. Other supervisors then play their roles one at a time with the same subordinate.

Step 4. Class Discussion

As a class, compare the different styles of interaction and leadership. Which ones were most effective?

Step 5. Shorter Role Plays (optional)

Divide class into pairs and have each person read one of the roles in a particular role play. Each pair does the role play and then the class discusses it. One group may be chosen to perform its role play in front of the whole class. How did your interaction compare with those done in front of the class? What seemed to work well in resolving the problem?

INSTRUCTIONS: FOR ROLE PLAY 4—CHRIS WILSON

Step 1. Introduction

Divide into groups of 8. Four should read the Chris Wilson role and the other four should each read one of the subordinate's roles—Paula Jaynes, Jim Lamp, Alice Pako, and Jack Kramer. (Change the names to match sexes if necessary.)

Step 2. First Run

Team up Wilson (A) with Paula Jaynes, Wilson (B) with Jim Lamp, etc. Play the roles.

Step 3. Second Run

Switch partners so that Wilson (A) is with Jim Lamp, Wilson (B) with Alice Pako, etc. Role-play. Do this up to three times, then every subordinate will have played the role four times with each Wilson.

Step 4. Group Discussion

In the groups of 8, discuss the different problem-solving styles. What would be best? Which leadership styles were most effective?

Step 5. Class Reports

Groups report interactions to the whole class.

---

* Adapted from Selter, Joseph, Interpersonal Communication/Conflict Role Plays. Used with permission.

Exercise 27

Prisoners' Dilemma:
An Intergroup Competition*

I. Purpose

(1) To explore trust between group members and the effects of betrayal of trust; (2) to demonstrate effects of interpersonal competition; and (3) to dramatize the merit of a collaborative posture in intragroup and intergroup relations.

II. Group Size

2 teams of no more than 8 members each.

III. Time Required

Approximately 1 hour. (Smaller teams take less time.)

IV. Preparation Required

Enough space for the two teams to meet separately without overhearing or disrupting each other.

V. Materials

Copies of the Prisoners' Dilemma Tally Sheet for all participants.

PROCESS

Step 1. Form Teams

Two teams are formed, Red and Blue. The teams are seated apart from each other. They are instructed not to communicate with the other team in any way, verbally or nonverbally, except when told to do so by the facilitator.

Step 2. Tally Sheets Distributed

Prisoners' Dilemma Tally Sheets are distributed to all participants. They are given time to study the directions. The facilitator then asks if there are any questions concerning the scoring.

Step 3. Round 1

Round 1 is begun. The facilitator tells the teams that they will have 3 minutes to make a team decision and instructs them not to write their decisions until that time is up.

Step 4. Scoring

The choices of the two teams are announced for Round 1. The scoring for that round is agreed upon and is entered on the scorecards.

Step 5. Rounds 2 and 3

Rounds 2 and 3 are conducted in the same way as Round 1.

Step 6. Round 4

Round 4 is announced as a special round, for which the payoff points are doubled. After representatives have conferred for 3 minutes, they return to their teams. Teams then have 3 minutes, as before, to make their decisions. When recording their scores, they should be reminded that points indicated by the payoff schedule are doubled for this round only.

Step 7. Rounds 5 through 8

Rounds 5 through 8 are conducted in the same manner as the first three rounds.

Step 8. Round 9

Round 9 is announced as a special round, in which the payoff points are "squared" (multiplied by themselves: e.g., a score of 4 would be $4^2=16$). A minus sign should be retained: (e.g. $-3^2=-9$). Team representatives meet for 3 minutes; then the teams meet for 5 minutes. At the facilitator's signal, the teams write their choices; then the two choices are announced.

Step 9. Round 10

Round 10 is handled exactly as Round 9. Payoff points are squared.

Step 10. Discussion

The entire group meets to process the experience. The point total for each team is announced, and the sum of the two team totals is calculated and compared to the maximum positive or negative outcomes (+126 or -126 points).

Variations

1. Process observers can be assigned to each team.

2. Teams can be placed in separate rooms, to minimize rule breaking.

3. The number of persons in each team can be varied.

4. In Round 10, each team can be directed to predict the choice of the other. These predictions can be posted before announcing the actual choices, as in the following diagram. (Actual choices are recorded in the circles after the predictions are announced.)

Predicting Team	*PREDICTED CHOICE*	
	Red Team	*Blue Team*
Red		
Blue		

PRISONERS' DILEMMA TALLY SHEET

Instructions: For 10 successive rounds, the Red Team will choose either an A or a B and the Blue Team will choose either an X or a Y. The score each team receives in a round is determined by the pattern made by the choices of both teams, according to the accompanying Payoff Schedule.

PAYOFF SCHEDULE

AX Both teams win 3 points.
AY Red Team loses 6 points; Blue Team wins 6 points.
BX Red Team wins 6 points; Blue Team loses 6 points.
BY Both teams lose 3 points.

SCORECARD

		CHOICE		*CUMULATIVE POINTS*	
Round	*Minutes*	*Red Team*	*Blue Team*	*Red Team*	*Blue Team*
1	3				
2	3				
3	3				
4[a]	3 (reps.) 3 (teams)				
5	3				
6	3				
7	3				
8	3				
9[b]	3 (reps.) 3 (teams)				
10[b]	3 (reps.) 3 (teams)				

[a] Payoff points are doubled for this round.
[b] Payoff points are squared for this round. (Retain the minus sign.)

---

* Reprinted from J. W. Pfeiffer and J. E. Jones (Eds.) *A Handbook of Structured Experiences for Human Relations Training, Vol. III.* San Diego, CA: Pfeiffer and Company, 1974. Used with permission.

10

STRATEGY

Exercise 28

A Question of Multinational Strategy and *You**

I. Purpose

The primary objective of this exercise is to reinforce an understanding of four types of corporate strategies in terms of the firm's market growth and market share. These four types were originally developed by the Boston Consulting Group, which they labeled "New Venture," "Star," "Dog," and "Cash Cow." Two secondary objectives of the exercise are to facilitate the development of a more detailed understanding of personal preferences for divisional management and a multinational point of view.

II. Group Size

Individually.

III. Time Required

10 to 15 minutes.

IV. Preparation Required

None, although the questionnaire may be assigned as an out-of-class activity.

V. Materials

None.

PROCESS

Step 1. The Scenario

Richard Tunnell is vice president of human resources for Spring Enterprises, Ltd. (SEL), a large multinational company that produces footwear (typically lightweight sandals) for one or more national markets using materials that are indigenous to, or at least specialties of, the region. Examples include yucca fiber in Latin America, leather in southern Europe, traditional carved wood in central Europe, and cotton in the southeastern United States. Corporate Headquarters of Spring Enterprises is located in a suburban area of Birmingham, England.

An immediate problem has been presented, indirectly, by you, the Carlstadt (New Jersey) divisional manager. The Carlstadt Division is a tiny, single-facility, production division that manufactures plastic sandals that are sold to large retail chain merchandisers for summer casual wear. These sandals are quite simple to make from the raw material of plastic foam boards and ribbon. Four presses cut out various sizes of soles from foam boards and the plastic ribbon is attached to the soles by a strong waterproof adhesive. One shift of four press operators, eight manual workers who cut ribbon and attach it to the soles, three packers, one warehouse supervisor, one office manager, and three accounting clerks constitute the work force of the division. All other business functions related to this product are performed by the regional home office staff, which is located in Wilmington, Delaware.

You are (your own plus 8) years old, have been with the company for only five years (three years in current position), yet are a highly valued divisional manager because of your ability to inspire divisional employees and meet home office objectives. Through the human resource professional grapevine, Tunnell has learned that you have been receiving inquiries from other companies about your availability should their company have an opening with more responsibility, greater career opportunity, and more pay.

SEL has a fairly fast promotion track for promising managers such as you and currently has a number of openings. Tunnell is convinced that it would be in the best interests of you, the company, and himself to assign you to another division, which, because of a larger work force, production, and sales, would also represent a promotion. And this is the situation that he presented to a management consultant friend over tea after watching the national team of England lose to the Italian national team in a World Cup qualifying match. Tunnell asks her for advice. She is an Italian and Tunnell, too bad, is British. For years she was a member of the staff of a well known Boston (U.S.) consulting firm; recently she opened her own consulting business specializing in multinational executive placement.

Step 2. Consultant Advice

After listening to Richard Tunnell's description of the situation, the consultant persuades him that the problem is one of matching your career interests with the appropriate divisional strategy. She has developed a simple question and answer form for situations such as these. The form does not provide specific answers, but it does help to point in the direction of a solution. It is to be filled out by the employee in question.

Step 3. The Form

Tunnell sends you the following form and explains that you are simply to distribute 5 points to each of the six pairs of statements; each pair consists of an a and b part. All 5 points must be allocated to each pair, hence, the possibilities are 0,5; 1,4; 2,3; 3,2; 4,1; 5,0. Other than the information presented in the scenario (step 1) you should base your answers on your own personal preferences.

1a. _____ I would prefer to manage a division with a small share of the market.

1b. _____ I would prefer to manage a division with a large share of the market.

Why did you distribute the points as you did in this pair?

_____

_____

_____

_____

2a. _____ I would prefer to manage a division with a fast growth rate.

2b. _____ I would prefer to manage a division with a slow growth rate.

Why did you distribute the points as you did in this pair?

_____

_____

_____

_____

3a. _____ I would prefer to manage a division with a high risk position.

3b. _____ I would prefer to manage a division with a low risk position.

Why did you distribute the points as you did in this pair?

_____

_____

_____

_____

4a. _____ I would prefer to manage a division with a high potential for divestment.

4a. _____ I would prefer to manage a division with a low potential for divestment.

Why did you distribute the points as you did in this pair?

_____

_____

_____

_____

5a. _____ I would prefer to manage a division with an expanding market.

5b. _____ I would prefer to manage a division with a mature market.

Why did you distribute the points as you did in this pair?

_____

_____

_____

_____

6a. _____ I would prefer to manage a division that generates capital primarily for the development of other divisions.

6b. _____ I would prefer to manage a division that generates capital primarily for its own development.

Why did you distribute the points as you did in this pair?

_____

_____

_____

_____

Step 4. Scaling Your Answers

Record the value you assigned to the statements as indicated in the following form. Note that one answer may be recorded several times in the form; this effect will be averaged through the entire exercise. When all blanks have been filled in, sum each of the four columns.

	I	II	III	IV
1a	___		___	
1b		___		___
2a		___		
2b	___		___	___
3a	___			
3b		___	___	___
4a			___	
4b	___	___		___
5a	___	___		
5b			___	___
6a				___
6b	___	___	___	
Total:	___	___	___	___

Step 5. Interpreting Your Answers

The following table was created by Richard Daft to portray the essential ideas of the four strategic perspectives developed by the Boston Consulting Group. The roman numeral in each cell of the table corresponds to the headings of the scaling chart of step 4. Another more detailed synopsis may be found in Bruce D. Henderson's book *Henderson on Management* (Englewood Cliffs, NJ: Prentice Hall, 1979, pp. 163-166).

CORPORATE STRATEGY FOR BUSINESS PORTFOLIO

	MARKET SHARE	
	Low	*High*
High **Market Growth** Low	I. **New Venture** Small share of expanding market. May be prize heifer or problem child.	II. **Star** Large share of expanding market. Rapid growth and expansion.
	III. **Dog** Small share of mature market. Consider divestment.	IV. **Cash Cow** Large share of mature market. Milk cash to fund new venture.

* Reprinted by permission from page 495 of *Organization Theory and Design* by
   R. L Daft; Copyright © 1989 by West Publishing Company. All rights reserved.

Exercise 29

Strategy, Stakeholders, and Social Responsibility*

I. Purpose

(1) To become familiar with the four strategic positions described by Miles and Snow; (2) to experience zero-sum decision making as individuals or as members of groups; (3) to develop an awareness of various stakeholder groups that are relevant to financial decisions of manufacturing organizations in the community; and (4) to experience the complexity of making operational and financial decisions with an awareness of the social responsibility of the firm.

II. Group Size

The project may be based on individual decision-making, group decision-making, or role playing within decision-making groups.

III. Time Required

50 to 75 minutes.

IV. Preparation Required

Read the material entitled "Miles and Snow's Four Strategic Types" at the end of the exercise or an alternative reading as indicated by your instructor.

V. Materials

None.

PROCESS

Step 1. Overview

1. Each student/group is given the authority, and charged with the responsibility, to allocate an extra $1 million to the projects listed in Table 29-1 in the amounts specified. Unallocated funds are lost and become unavailable to the student/group.

2. The student/group will be instructed to role-play this allocation decision in correspondence with one of the four strategic types as described by Miles and Snow.

Step 2. Group Formation

If the exercise is to be based on group work, students will be advised to form groups of "plant management personnel" which will make decisions as to the relative amounts to allocate to the various projects indicated in the table. Group members may be asked to play specific plant management roles.

Step 3. Exercise Scenario

You are the plant manager (or a member of the plant management group) for a small manufacturing plant that has developed (i.e., the instructor has assigned) one particular strategic approach (defender, prospector, reactor, or analyzer).

You have the authority to allocate funds as you deem appropriate. However, you also must be able to justify your decisions to top management, your employees, the community, and other interested people *from the perspective of the strategic approach that has been developed (assigned).*

Although the plant has been operating at an acceptable level, there is always the need to improve operations. You have argued that with extra funding, you could make significant improvements in the plant's operations. The company has given you the opportunity to prove the merit of your ideas by allocating an extra $1 million to your budget. The only conditions are that:

1. You must spend the money for the projects listed in the table.

2. You must spend, for each project, at least the amount listed under the first column (from the left) and you may spend only the amounts listed.

3. You may have to justify your allocation decisions to a committee of managers, employees, and other members of the business community.

4. Any money you do not spend must be returned to the parent company and is lost to you.

Step 4. Consider Alternatives

Project Trade-Off Alternatives

Project	Alternative A	Alternative B	Alternative C
Market research	Maintain current market share Cost $50,000	Study penetration of national market Cost $200,000	Explore options international business Cost $300,000
Dividends	Pay none Cost $0	Pay $.50 per share Cost $150,000	Pay $1 per share and attract investors Cost $300,000
Wage increases	Maintain current levels Cost $0	Give 5% cost of living increase Cost $150,000	Give cost of living and 5% merit Cost $300,000
Pollution control	Kill everything within 1 mile Cost $0	Comply with new legislation Cost $150,000	Significantly reduce pollution Cost $250,000
Discrimination	Hire qualified white males and risk a discrimination suit Cost $140,000	Hire token minorities and hope for the best Cost $250,000	Hire "hard-core" unemployed and train and generate much goodwill Cost $350,000
Research and development	Leave well enough alone Cost $0	Research means of reducing manufacturing costs Cost $150,000	Seek ways to increase brand loyalty Cost $250,000
Enhanced public image	Host wine and cheese party for local officials Cost $10,000	Hold weekend retreat for major stockholders Cost $150,000	Rent resort for a week to gain support of major financial institutions Cost $250,000
Compensation	Money is unimportant Pay self $0	Pay self $50,000 in salary and fringe benefits	Pay self $100,000

Step 5. Make Decisions Concerning Financial Allocations

Market research $ _____

Dividends $ _____

Wage increases $ _____

Pollution control $ _____

Discrimination $ _____

Research and development $ _____

Enhanced public image $ _____

Compensation: $ _____

MILES AND SNOW'S FOUR STRATEGIC TYPES

Raymond Miles and Charles Snow classify organizations—based on the rate at which they change their products or markets—into one of four strategic types: defenders, prospectors, analyzers, and reactors. While their discussion centers on business firms, the categories they use probably have their counterpart in nonprofit organizations as well.

Defenders seek stability by producing only a limited set of products directed at a narrow segment of the total potential market. Within this limited niche, or domain, defenders strive aggressively to prevent competitors from entering their "turf." Organizations do this through standard economic actions such as competitive pricing or production of high-quality products. But defenders tend to ignore developments and trends outside their domains, choosing instead to grow through market penetration and perhaps some limited product development. There is little or no scanning of the environment to find new areas of opportunity, but there is intensive planning oriented toward cost and other efficiency issues. The result is a structure made up of high horizontal differentiation, centralized control, and an elaborate formal hierarchy for communications. Over time, true defenders are able to carve out and maintain small niches within their industries that are difficult for competitors to penetrate. An example of a defender strategy is the manufacturer of Soft-Soap. The company has chosen a narrow domain—the liquid hand and body soap market—and hopes to fend off competitors such as Proctor & Gamble by promoting aggressively and developing a narrow range of similar products.

Prospectors are almost the opposite of defenders. Their strength is finding and exploiting new-product and market opportunities. Innovation may be more important than high profitability. This describes, for instance, several magazine publishers who introduce new magazine titles almost monthly, constantly attempting to identify new market segments. It would also be the appropriate label for an organization like 3M. That company has built its reputation and long-term profitability on developing innovative products, getting quickly to the market with those products, exploiting opportunities while they are still innovative, and then getting out.

The prospector's success depends on developing and maintaining the capacity to survey a wide range of environmental conditions, trends, and events. Therefore, prospectors invest heavily in personnel who scan the environment for potential opportunities. Since flexibility is critical to prospectors, the structure will also be flexible. It will rely on multiple technologies that have a low degree of routinization and mechanization. There will be numerous decentralized units. The structure will be low in formalization, have decentralized control, with lateral as well as vertical communications. "In short, the prospector is effective if it can respond to the demands of tomorrow's world. To the extent that the world of tomorrow is similar to that of today, the prospector cannot maximize profitability because of its inherent inefficiency."

Analyzers try to capitalize on the best of both the preceding types. They seek to minimize risk and maximize opportunity for profit. Their strategy is to move into new products or new markets only after viability has been proved by prospectors. Analyzers live by imitation. They take the successful ideas of prospectors and copy them. Manufacturers of mass-marketed fashion goods that are rip-offs of designer styles follow the analyzer strategy. This label also probably characterizes such well-known firms as Digital Equipment Corporation, IBM, and Caterpillar. They essentially follow their smaller and more innovative competitors with superior products, but only after their competitors have demonstrated that the market is there.

Analyzers must have the ability to respond to the lead of key prospectors, yet at the same time maintain operating efficiency in their stable product and market areas. Analyzers will tend to have smaller profit margins in the products and services that they sell than will prospectors, but they are more efficient. Prospectors have to have high margins to justify the risks that they take and their productive inefficiencies.

Analyzers seek both flexibility and stability. They respond to these goals by developing a structure made up of dual components. Parts of these organizations have high levels of standardization, routinization, and mechanization for efficiency. Other parts are adaptive, to enhance flexibility. In this way, they seek structures that can accommodate both stable and dynamic areas of operation. But in this compromise there can be costs. If situations change rapidly, demanding that organizations move fully in either direction, their ability to take such action is severely limited.

Reactors represent a residual strategy. The label is meant to describe the inconsistent and unstable patterns that arise when one of the other three strategies is pursued improperly. In general, reactors respond inappropriately, perform poorly, and as a result are reluctant to commit themselves aggressively to a specific strategy for the future. What can cause this? Top management may have failed to make the organization's strategy clear. Management may not have fully shaped the organization's strategy structure to fit the chosen strategy. Management may have maintained its current strategy-structure relationship despite overwhelming changes in environmental conditions. Whatever the reason, however, the outcome is the same. The organization lacks a set of response mechanisms with which to face a change environment.

* Adapted from Thomas, J. G. (1992), Examining Social Responsibility: A Trade-Off Among Stakeholders. *Journal of Management Education*, 16(2), 250-253. Stephen P. Robbins, *Organization Theory: Structure, Design, and Applications*, 3rd ed., 1990, pp. 130-133. Reprinted by permission of Prentice Hall, Englewood Cliffs, New Jersey.

Exercise 30

Organizational Conversion Strategy in Higher Education: Two Years to Four*

I. Purpose

(1) To review and evaluate the performance of Florence College, a fictionalized but close to real life, two-year, upper division (junior/senior level) college, for the purpose of designing a four-year undergraduate college structure; (2) to reconstruct, clarify, and affirm the long-term mission of Florence College; and (3) to prepare objectives and action steps for major efforts of Florence College for the next year.

II. Group Size

8 to 12 persons who make up the top management of Florence College, including the president.

III. Time Required

Two class meetings of 50 to 75 minutes each. A third class meeting, or longer class meeting times, would be desirable but not absolutely necessary.

IV. Preparation Required

One large room furnished with a work table, chairs, and easels for newsprint (or transparency projectors for handwritten transparencies). Smaller rooms similarly furnished, for individual or small group work, would be helpful but not necessary.

V. Materials

(1) At least six copies of the Reviewing Objectives and Strategies Sheet for each participant (one is provided at the end of this exercise).

(2) Newsprint tablet, masking tape, and easel, *or* transparency sheets and projector, for each group.

(3) Set of newsprint, *or* transparency, markers.

PROCESS

Step 1. Introduction

The instructor reviews the goals of the activity and indicates that these goals will serve as the agenda for at least two class meetings.

Step 2. Data Search and Compilation

Understanding that planning must be based on data, the group obtains (through direct research activity and instructor-provided documents) information about Florence College's performance, structure, and strategy for the past several years.

Step 3. Assessment of Positive Outcomes

Once the information about Florence College has been obtained, the group should engage in brainstorming and developing answers to the question "What positive accomplishments have been achieved in the past several years?"

Among the items to consider are such things as size, growth, revenues, new organizational structures, new policies, new personnel, new technical resources, new linkages to outside groups, impact on the community, events, awards, and new learnings. All answers are listed on newsprint (or transparency sheets) and then the list is reviewed to eliminate redundancies and nonpertinent items.

Step 4. Assessment of Negative Outcomes

The brainstorming procedure is repeated for the question "What have been Florence College's failures or shortcomings during the past several years?"

Step 5. Assessment of Mission

The group should assess the language of the Florence College mission statement by considering the following points:

1. The management team should be clear about, and in agreement with, Florence College's mission.

2. All activities of Florence College should help to achieve its mission.

3. A mission statement may be a detailed phrase, a few sentences, or a lengthy document.

Step 6. New Mission Statement

At this point the group should state Florence College's mission in a few sentences. All should agree in essence with this mission statement. Guidelines for creating a mission statement are

1. State a goal rather than operations. A mission is more related to purpose than it is to activities.

2. A statement can be too broad or too narrow, thus limiting its usefulness. Avoid high-sounding generalities as well as specifics.

3. The statement should distinguish Florence College from others.

4. Throughout the discussion, be alert to problems of interpretation or emphasis and strive to clarify and rationalize these differences.

Step 7. Preparing Objectives and Action Steps

In order to prepare objectives and action steps for the next year, several activities are involved. First, the participants will work individually on familiar material that they have gathered. Second, the group members will work together in planning new efforts. Third, the Reviewing Objectives and Strategies Sheet should be completed. The emphasis of the activity is on quantity of ideas rather than on technicalities; an objective is simply a statement of *intention*, whereas strategies are statements of steps that one will take to reach objectives.

Step 8. Preparing a Florence College Organization Chart

On the basis of the work completed thus far, construct a Florence College organization chart. This chart should portray all lines of authority among categories of managers, functional relationships among employees and departments, and a guide to courses of study.

Step 9. Presenting the Mission Statement, Objectives, Action Steps, and Organization Chart

Using either the newsprint easel *or* the transparency projector, present the conclusions of your group as to the mission, objectives, action steps, and Organization chart for the new four-year Florence College.

REVIEWING OBJECTIVES AND STRATEGIES

1. **Objective(s)** (What is your intention? What do you plan to achieve? What end result do you want?)

   _____

   _____

   _____

   _____

2. **Strategies** (What action steps will be necessary to reach the objective(s)? If you are not the person to take these steps, identify the person who is.)

   _____

   _____

   _____

   _____

3. **Who will be responsible?**

_____

_____

_____

_____

4. **Resources needed** (If money or people or other resources are needed for this item, indicate them here.)

_____

_____

_____

_____

---

* Reprinted from J. W. Pfeiffer and L. D. Goodstein (eds.), *The 1982 Annual for Facilitators, Trainers, and Consultants.* San Diego, CA: Pfeiffer and Company, 1982. Used with permission.

11

SIZE

Exercise 31

How "Big" Is Your College?*

I. Purpose

To examine the various definitions of organizational size.

II. Group Size

Complete exercise individually; hold small group discussion of conclusions.

III. Time Required

1 hour; may be decreased by assigning exercise for out-of-class.

IV. Preparation Required

None.

V. Materials

None.

PROCESS

Step 1. Compare Colleges

Review the comparison chart of various college characteristics.

Step 2. Select the "Biggest" College

Step 3. Group Choice

Compare your choice with those of other class members. Attempt to reconcile differences and arrive at a group consensus.

VARIATION

Step 1. Add Your College

Collect data about your own college and include it in the comparison. (Use a reference like *Peterson's Guide to Four-Year Colleges* to obtain data for your school.)

	College A	College B	College C	College D	Your College
Total enrollment	28,512	13,857	34,361	10,000	
Undergraduate enrollment	21,116	8,584	25,780	7,600	
Land area	405 a	260 a	2,000 a	1,250 a	
Funded endowments	$43.3M	$183.3M	$268,420	$652M	
Research expenditures	$51M	$71.4M	$223.3M	$28.9M	
Total faculty	1,526	1,615	2,660	820	
Full-time faculty	1,374	1,097	2,470	620	
Part-time faculty	152	518	190	200	
Total freshmen	2,996	1,790	3,174	1,880	
Acceptance percentage	72%	80%	66%	49%	
National Merit Scholar finalists	53	27	130	150	
National Merit Scholars	53	27	130	15	
Library volumes	1.98M	1.7M	2.9M	1.9M	
Periodicals	18,436	15,900	27,800	20,230	
Acquisition expenditures	$3.9M	$4.9M	$14.6M	$9.8M	
Computers	70	200	947	444	
Computer expenditures	$12.9M	$5.5M	$15.1M	$5.3M	
Housing spaces	3,900	4,188	6,419	6,400	
Placement Office expenditures $	$543,000	$321,917	$709,943	$400,000	
Ranking					

* Stephen P. Robbins, *Organization Theory: Structure, Design and Applications,* 1990, pp. 170-171. Reprinted by permission of Prentice Hall, Englewood Cliffs, New Jersey.

Exercise 32

Intertwine: Intergroup Collaboration*

I. Purpose

(1) To illustrate intergroup task interdependence; (2) to explore aspects of organizational size as it affects communication and division of labor; and (3) to practice intergroup problem-solving skills.

II. Group Size

2, 4, 6, 8, or 10 triads.

III. Time Required

Approximately 1 hour.

IV. Preparation Required

None.

V. Materials

1. A copy of the Intertwine Observation Sheet for each observer.

2. One packet of prepared twine. The packet should contain three-pieces *each* of three different *types* of rope, twine, or string—a total of nine pieces. The length of each piece should be 3 feet multiplied by the number of triads, up to approximately 20 feet. (For example, three pieces may be thin, white string; three may be rough, red

twine; and three may be thicker, tan rope. The three types should vary in more than one obvious way.) All nine pieces are to be tangled together (but not knotted) prior to the activity.

3. Newsprint and a felt-tipped marker.

PROCESS

Step 1. Task Definition

The group is to work on a problem-solving task. The participants are divided into triads (groups of 3 members each). Additional participants are designated as observers.

Step 2. Physical Arrangement

The triads arrange themselves in parallel rows (or two concentric circles) so that the rows face each other, as illustrated in the accompanying diagrams. The triads will remain in these positions throughout the activity.

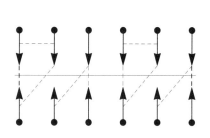 **or**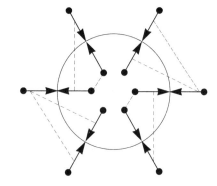

Step 3. Observer Assignment

Each observer is given a copy of the Intertwine Observation Sheet.

Step 4. Task Preparation

The tangled twine is laid on the floor lengthwise between the two rows of participants.

Step 5. The Task

With the twine stretched out lengthwise between the rows, each participant is to hold a portion of all three pieces of one of the types of twine, that is, a portion of all three tan strands or all three red strands, etc., with each member of the triad holding a different type of twine. (The participant's task is not to gather up all three pieces of each type, but to hold a *portion* of the full length of twine.)

Step 6. The Rule

No two adjacent people, either within or between triads, may hold the same type of twine.

Step 7. Reactions

Discuss your individual and group reactions to the activity. Use the following items to facilitate your discussion:

1. The relationship between the task and the need for collaboration

2. Aspects of collaboration such as communication processes and division of labor

3. The differences between intergroup problem solving and intragroup problem solving

4. Other learning related to task interdependence among groups

---

* Reprinted from J. W. Pfeiffer and L. D. Goodstein (eds.). *The 1982 Annual for Facilitators, Trainers, and Consultants.* San Diego, CA: Pfeiffer and Company, 1982. Used with permission.

Exercise 33

Building Blocks and Slogans: A Matter of Size*

I. Purpose

To provide an opportunity to experience the effect of group size on routine and creative activities company activities in terms of (1) formalization/standardization, (2) decentralization/delegation, and (3) subunit size. A secondary purpose is to enable the students to develop a sense of subgroup identity despite the instructor's "random" group membership assignment.

II. Group Size

Ideally, three very different group sizes would be formed, with as many of each size level as total enrollment will permit.

III. Time Required

40 to 75 minutes.

IV. Preparation Required

None.

V. Materials

One pair of scissors, one roll of cellophane/masking tape, and 26 sheets of construction paper (several colors if possible) for each group.

PROCESS

Step 1. Form Groups

The instructor will assign you to a group on, essentially, a random basis. One member of the group will be designated as the "quality control specialist" (QCS), and the task of this person will be to record the time taken for each phase and to serve as a general observer and recorder of decisions made by the group.

Step 2. Create a Name for Your Company

The name for your toy block manufacturing company should be reflective of the individuals in the group, attractive to future consumers (purchasers of toy blocks for children) and consist of *one* differentiating word. Words and phrases such as: "Inc.," "And Sons," "Company," "Family Enterprises Ltd." do not count as part of the one word.

Step 3. Toy Block Production

In this step the group is to produce 26 paper blocks, one for each letter of the alphabet, using the pattern provided. Each of the six sides of a block will be marked with the same (uppercase form) letter. Specifically the following tasks are involved: (a) *trace* the block onto each of the 26 sheets of construction paper; (b) *cut* out each block; (c) *write* letters on all six sides of all 26 cutouts; (d) *fold* each cutout into cube shape; (e) *tape* each block into a relatively permanent cube.

Step 4. Company Slogan Creation

Here the objective is to arrange the blocks into words that will form a slogan for your company. In this particular industry, long slogans are usually more effective; obviously, a letter may only be used once. A starting point would be the name of the company—hoping to develop a strong brand association on the part of employees, customers (large retail merchandisers), consumers, and owners.

Step 5. Slogan Visual Design

The last step is to arrange the words of the slogan in a physical vertical hierarchy for use as a trademark and visual identification for the company. One such hierarchy would be triangular—smaller words at the top and larger words at the bottom—but the collective imagination of the group should be the guide here. By all means, the blocks would be taped together in a fairly sturdy structure. See the sample slogan for an elementary example; your group should be able to do much better!

Step 6. Organizational Assessment

Refer to the Organizational Assessment Instrument and, in combination with the documentation provided by the QCS, assess each of the seven items listed. One summary assessment should be developed for each group.

Step 7. Discussion

Using the questions provided by the instructor or another source, discuss the relative influence of size on the activities and experiences within the groups.

ALPHABET BLOCK DESIGN PATTERN

SAMPLE SLOGAN

OWN	ALPHA	CUBES	KID

ORGANIZATIONAL ASSESSMENT INSTRUMENT

Name of Your Organization (Total Member Size)

	Block Making	*Slogan Making*	*Visual Making*
Elapsed time			
Decentralization			
Formalization			
Human resource management			
Difficult aspects			
Easy aspects			
Subunit number/ size			

---

* Reprinted from J. W. Pfeiffer and L. D. Goodstein (eds.). *The 1982 Annual for Facilitators, Trainers, and Consultants.* San Diego, CA: Pfeiffer and Company, 1982. Used with permission.

12

DECISION MAKING

Exercise 34

Led Like Sheep:
Task-Related Decision Making*

I. **Purpose**

   To demonstrate the differences in group decision-making approaches related to differences in the tasks to be accomplished.

II. **Group Size**

   Groups of 3 to 7 members each.

III. **Time Required**

   75 to 90 minutes.

IV. **Preparation Required**

   None.

V. **Materials**

   List of words; algebraic matrices.

PROCESS

Step 1. Group Formation

Form a group with no more than 7 and no less than 3 members.

Step 2. Task Completion

As a group, complete each of the four tasks as assigned by the instructor. Your group will have a total of 20 minutes in which to complete all four tasks. Your group may use any available references.

Step 3. Compare Decisions

Group decisions are compared and, when appropriate, the correct answer given.

Step 4. Discussion

Relate observations about your group relative to group characteristics (cohesiveness, norms, leadership, accuracy, speed, risk taking, creativity, size, composition) and group processes (communication patterns, resource allocation, decision making).

TASKS

Task 1: Identify the listed paired words as antonyms or synonyms.

Task 2: Generate words that rhyme with the word provided.

Task 3: Arrive at the product of two matrices provided.

Task 4: Provide the best route between two cities, provided by your instructor.

---

* Adapted from Dodd-McCue, D. (1991). Led Like Sheep: An Exercise for Linking Group Decision Making to Different Types of Tasks. *Journal of Managerial Education*, 15 (3), pp. 335-339.

Exercise 35

Maximizing or Satisficing:
Pick the Best—
Or the First Good One?*

I. Purpose

This exercise demonstrates a decision-making problem; whether you can make the "best" choice of alternatives or you choose the first good one to come along. This is the difference between *maximizing* and *satisficing*. *Maximizing* is choosing the best alternative. *Satisficing* is choosing the first available alternative that meets the minimum requirements a decision maker sets. Maximizing can be accomplished when we know all possible alternatives. Satisficing is done when we are not aware of all the alternatives. Many decisions are "satisficing" choices. For example, in choosing the best spouse, it would be necessary to know all the people that we might marry. Unfortunately, potential spouses, do not come in bunches but rather, at best, a few at a time. Someone better might come along later. But what if he or she doesn't? When do we find someone "good enough" to marry? Can we wait for the right person? Job choice is much the same way. We don't have the luxury of knowing about all jobs at the same time, so that we can choose the best one. Often we have to make a decision, choosing from among those that we have—and hope it is a good one.

II. Group Size

Individually.

III. Time Required

Approximately 10 minutes.

IV. Preparation Required

None.

V. Materials

None.

PROCESS

When instructed, read the following situational description and place yourself in the role of Connie Heerman, a staff assistant to Betty Ewing, president of Ewing Manufacturing, a rapidly growing, medium-sized manufacturer of commercial air-conditioning equipment.

SITUATION DESCRIPTION—PART A

Ewing Manufacturing has decided to discontinue its practice of contracting out its computer and data processing work. Betty Ewing, the president, has decided to purchase a computer system. As staff assistant to the president, you have been charged with evaluating the various systems and making a recommendation as to what computer should be purchased. Ewing's computer needs are very specialized. Regular equipment will not work. The regular computer manufacturers produce these special computers infrequently and the demand is very high. It is a seller's market.

You have contacted eight computer manufacturers and given all of them identical specifications. You find out that these manufacturers will call you when a machine becomes available. Each will quote you a price for a unit that will precisely meet your needs, but these quotes will come in one at a time. You have made some estimates and believe that $500,000, plus or minus $20,000, will be the cost.

Several suppliers have informed you that they *may* call you within the next three weeks with a price. You will be given a one-time price and you will have 48 hours to accept or reject the offer. If you reject the offer, the computer manufacturer will sell the equipment to another customer. If you accept it, you will receive no other offers. If you reject an offer, you may get some additional ones, but you do *not* know how many quotes you will receive. Since you must have this equipment, you will have to take the last offer regardless of price, if you did not agree earlier to purchase one of the units.

You will now start receiving the bids. After each bid is made, place the name of the company and the price in the appropriate column. Then decide whether or not you accept the offer. Write your acceptance or rejection in the column on the right. Remember the proposals come several days apart, and when you turn one down (with the exception of the last one), it will be rescinded.

	Company	Offer	Accept or Reject
1.			
2.			
3.			
4.			
5.			
6.			
7.			
8.			

SITUATION DESCRIPTION—PART B

Now that you have the computer, you become aware of several new applications for Ewing Manufacturing. With the addition of an on-line, high-speed printer, you estimate that you can significantly improve productivity.

There are several units that seem to meet your needs, according to your research. Most of them have the capability to produce at the level you want. However, there are some differences with respect to durability and maintenance.

When you ask the manufacturers for bids, you receive them from only three of the firms. They are identical bids from each manufacturer. There are some differences between machines with respect to the cost and frequency of repair. The printers from which you can choose are listed below, with a brief rating of their maintenance records:

Acme Printer. This unit has acceptable performance capability. It has a rating of .25, which is the probability that it will experience a major breakdown within the next three years.

Brilliant Writer. This unit is equally adequate. Its maintenance rating is .20, the probability of a major breakdown within three years.

Clear Writer. This has the same performance capacity as the Acme and the Brilliant; the three-year maintenance rating is .10. Of all machines it is the most dependable.

1. What other information do you need to make a good choice?_____

_____

_____

_____

a.   Basic cost of printer:

Acme Printer   _____

Brilliant Writer   _____

Clear Writer   _____

b.   Compute expected cost of breakdown

Printer	Breakdown Cost		Probability of Breakdown		Expected Cost of Breakdown
Acme Printer	_____	X	_____	=	_____
Brilliant Writer	_____	X	_____	=	_____
Clear Writer	_____	X	_____	=	_____

c.   Total cost computation (transfer the appropriate figures above to the table below)

Printer	Basic Cost		Expected Breakdown Cost		Total Cost
Acme Printer	_____	+	_____	=	_____
Brilliant Writer	_____	+	_____	=	_____
Clear Writer	_____	+	_____	=	_____

      d.   Which one is best?_____

2.   Are there any circumstances under which you might purchase the Clear Writer, regardless of cost?   ❏ Yes   ❏ No

      What are they? _____

_____

_____

---

* Adapted from Tosi, H.L. & Young, J.W. (1982). Decision Making Exercise 26. *Management: Experiences and Demonstrations*. Homewood, IL: Richard D. Irwin, Inc., pp. 159-164.

Exercise 36

Winter Survival*

I. Purpose

To compare the effectiveness of several different methods of making decisions.

II. Group Size

Groups of 6 to 8 members each.

III. Time Required

1 hour.

IV. Preparation Required

None.

V. Materials

Instructions for observers; a description of the situation and a decision form; a group summary sheet; a summary table.

PROCESS

Step 1. Form Groups

Form groups of approximately 8 members; 6 participants, and 2 observers. Each group will be assigned a number for purposes of identification. Read the situation.

Step 2. Individual Completion

Complete the decision form quietly and individually. You will have 15 minutes to complete the decision form.

Step 3. Consensus Guidelines

Your group is to employ the method of group consensus in reaching its decision. This means that the ranking for each of the 12 survival items *must* be agreed upon by each group member before it becomes a part of the group decision. Consensus is difficult to reach. Therefore, not every ranking will meet with everyone's complete approval. Try, as a group, to make each ranking one with which all group members can at least partially agree. Here are some guidelines to use in reaching consensus:

1. Avoid arguing blindly for your own opinions. Present your position as clearly and logically as possible, but listen to other members' reactions and consider them carefully before you press your point.

2. Avoid changing your mind just to reach agreement and avoid conflict. Support only solutions with which you are able to agree to at least some degree. Yield only to positions that have objective and logically sound foundations.

Step 4. Group Ranking

The groups have 45 minutes to decide on a group ranking of the items on the decision form. Make a copy of the group ranking with your group designation clearly written on the top.

Step 5. Scoring

Score the individual decision forms in the following way:

1. Score the net difference between the participant's answer and the correct answer. For example, if the participant's answer was 9 and the correct answer is 12, the net difference is 3. Disregard all plus or minus signs; find only the net difference for each item.

2. Total these scores; the result is the participant's score. The lower the score, the more accurate the ranking.

3. To arrive at an average member score, total all members' scores for each group and divide by the number of members.

4. Put the scores in order from best to worst for each group. This ranking will be used to compare how many members, if any, had more accurate scores than the group's score.

5. In the summary table that follows the instruction sheets for the groups, enter the average member's score for each group and the score of the most accurate group member.

Step 6. Correct Ranking

Correct ranking provided.

Step 7. Group Discussion

Here are some questions the group might discuss:

1. How well did the group use its resources? Was there anyone who had valuable information who could not persuade others to his or her point of view? If so, why? How were silent members treated by the group? Were they encouraged to participate or left alone?

2. What factors caused the group to use its resources well or not well? Who behaved in what ways to influence group functioning?

3. Was there anyone who forced his or her opinion on the group? If so, why was he or she able to do this?

4. Did the group follow its instructions in making decisions? What influence did the instructions have on the way the group functioned?

5. What were the personal reactions of one particular group member to the group decision making? How did this person feel? What was he or she thinking?

6. How similar were the behaviors in this exercise to those in other group sessions? What implications does this exercise have for group meetings?

Step 8. Class Discussion

Share the conclusions of each group in a general session.

INSTRUCTIONS TO OBSERVERS

This exercise looks at the process by which groups make decisions. Crucial issues are how well the group uses the resources of its members, how much commitment to implement the decision is mustered, how the future decision-making ability of the group is affected, and how members feel about and react to what is taking place. As an observer, you may wish to focus on the following issues:

1. Who does and does not participate in the discussion? Who participates the most?

2. Who influences the decision and who does not? How is influence determined (expertise, sex, loudness of voice)?

3. Who is involved and who is uninvolved?

4. What are the dominant feelings of the group members? How would you describe the group atmosphere during the meeting?

5. What leadership behaviors are present and absent in the group?

6. What are the basic causes for the members' resources being used or not being used?

WINTER SURVIVAL: THE SITUATION

Your university soccer team has just crash-landed in the woods of northern Minnesota and southern Manitoba. It is 11:32 A.M. in mid-January. The light plane in which you were traveling crashed on a lake. The pilot and copilot were killed. Shortly after the crash, the plane sank completely into the lake with the pilot's and copilot's bodies inside. None of you are seriously injured and you are all dry.

The crash came suddenly, before the pilot had time to radio for help or inform anyone of your position. Because your pilot was trying to avoid a storm, you know the plane was considerably off course. The pilot announced shortly before the crash that you were 20 miles northwest of a small town that is the nearest known habitation.

You are in a wilderness area made up of thick woods broken by many lakes and streams. The snow depth varies from above the ankles in windswept areas to knee-deep where it has drifted. The last weather report indicated that the temperature would reach -25°F in the daytime and -40°F night. There is plenty of dead wood and twigs in the immediate area. You are dressed in winter clothing appropriate for city wear—suits, pantsuits, street shoes, and overcoats.

While escaping from the plane, several members of your group salvaged 12 items. Your task is to rank these items according to their importance to your survival, starting with 1 for the most important item and ending with 12 for the least important one.

You may assume that the number of passengers is the same as the number of persons in your group, and that the group has agreed to stick together.

WINTER SURVIVAL DECISION FORM

Rank the following items according to their importance to your survival, starting with 1 for the most important one and 12 for the least important one.

_3_ Ball of steel wool

_7_ Newspapers (one per person)

_11_ Compass

_10_ Hand ax

_1_ Cigarette lighter (without fluid)

_9_ Loaded .45-caliber pistol

_12_ Sectional air map made of plastic

_4_ Twenty-by-twenty-foot piece of heavy-duty canvas

_2_ Extra shirt and pants for each survivor

_6_ Can of shortening

_8_ Quart of 100-proof whiskey

_5_ Family-size chocolate bar (one per person)

WINTER SURVIVAL: GROUP SUMMARY SHEET

Item	MEMBERS						Summary
	1	*2*	*3*	*4*	*5*	*6*	
Ball of steel wool							
Newspapers							
Compass							
Hand ax							
Cigarette lighter							
.45-caliber pistol							
Sectional air map							
Canvas							
Shirt and pants							
Shortening							
Whiskey							
Chocolate bars							

SUMMARY TABLE: ACCURACY OF DECISIONS

Group	BEFORE GROUP DISCUSSION		AFTER GROUP DECISION			
	Average member's score	*Most accurate member's score*	*Consensus-Group score*	*Gain or loss over average member's score*	*Gain or loss over most accurate member's score*	*Number of members superior to group score*
1						
2						
3						
4						

* Adapted from Johnson, D. W. & Johnson, F. P. (1982). Winter Survival Exercise. *Joining Together: Group Theory & Group Skills.* Englewood Cliffs, NJ: Prentice Hall, pp. 111-118.

NOTES

NOTES

NOTES

NOTES